# The Route Map to Business Continuity Management

# The Route Map to Business Continuity Management

Meeting the Requirements of **BS 25999**

John Sharp

Business
Information

First published in the UK in 2008
by
BSI
389 Chiswick High Road
London W4 4AL

Reprinted 2008

Typeset in Frutiger by Monolith – http://www.monolith.uk.com
Printed in Great Britain by MPG Books, Bodmin, Cornwall

*British Library Cataloguing in Publication Data*
A catalogue record for this book is available from the British Library

ISBN 978-0-580-50952-0

# Contents

# Contents

## Contents

# Foreword

For many years robust business continuity has been regarded as a rather nebulous subject. One organization's idea of robustness did not necessarily meet with another's. Advice could be sought from industry experts but both methodologies and outcomes could vary considerably. Organizations concerned about vulnerabilities in their supply chain could ask their key suppliers for details of their plans, and could even attend plan exercises, but had no dependable way of measuring effectiveness. There was little in the way of a consistent approach, causing difficulty and confusion for those creating plans as well as those evaluating them.

Insurers have long recognized the value of good business continuity planning, which demonstrated active risk management and helped mitigate the financial effects of business interruptions. However, in the absence of a common approach it has been very difficult for organizations to demonstrate to insurers in a universally recognized way that their process is, indeed, robust. That all changed with the publication of BS 25999-1 in 2006. This book provides guidance and a route map to good practice business continuity management (BCM) based on the British Standard.

Part 1 of BS 25999 establishes the process, principles and terminology of BCM good practice, while Part 2, due to be published in late 2007, defines the specification for formally assessing an organization's BCM ability. Aon's Risk Control Consultants were delighted to be represented on the committee that formulated this British Standard and Aon is actively encouraging the insurance market to adopt it as their default standard. This will lead to enhanced capability to respond to adverse situations and the ability to demonstrate this to all interested parties.

The new Standard provides a consistent approach and this book gives practical help on meeting the requirements for those charged with developing BCM, regardless of the size or sector of their organization.

When Aon was asked to be associated with this publication we saw it as an excellent opportunity to support a book, which we believe will be of great assistance to those organizations setting out on the road towards robust BCM, or seeking to make improvements to their existing BCM processes. Also, it has enabled us to confirm and demonstrate our ongoing support for the British Standard and the effect that this will have in raising standards of BCM.

John Sharp has been influential in developing the profession and practice of BCM both in the UK and overseas. He has participated in Aon seminars and I know has been a source of inspiration to both our clients and our staff alike with his enthusiasm, knowledge and practicality. This book reflects that approach and we are delighted to give it our support.

Michael Brooks
Head of Operational Risk Management
Commercial Insurance
Aon Limited

# Preface

This book has been written to help those managers who, for whatever reason, have decided to introduce BCM (business continuity management) into their organization. It is based on Parts 1 and 2 of the new British Standard for BCM, BS 25999, and on the Plan, Do, Check, Act model used by BS 25999-2 and other management systems, such as the quality management systems Standard, BS EN ISO 9001:2000.

The book includes brief case studies to illustrate the main ideas of business continuity management, and templates to assist with the various stages of the BCM process.

Those seeking to implement BCM are encouraged to build on what already exists in their organization, e.g. IT recovery plans, risk management, security and personal succession planning. They are further encouraged to involve representatives from all departments and support functions to achieve a uniform approach to BCM and a more resilient organization.

# 1. Introduction

BCM (business continuity management) is a relatively new management discipline that has become increasingly important given the turbulent environments in which organizations now find themselves.

Terrorist activities, extremes of climate, failure of utilities, disruption in supply chains and the threat of human and animal pandemics are just some examples of major events that can result in widespread disruptions to communities, resulting in the failure of organizations to deliver their products and services.

It is not just major events that can cause a break in continuity of operations. One in five UK organizations suffer a disruptive event every year caused by lower-level incidents such as fire, sickness, loss of technology, denial of site access or loss of a key supplier. These events may not impact on the wider community but could lead to the failure of an individual organization through loss of customers and disruption to cash flow. By adopting business continuity management, organizations will be better equipped to meet the challenges they face when disrupted for whatever reason.

In 2003 the British Standards Institution published a Publicly Available Specification, PAS 56, *Guide to business continuity management*, which drew together the best practice in BCM and was adopted by many organizations throughout the world.

In 2006 PAS 56 was withdrawn and replaced by a new British Standard for BCM: BS 25999-1. This is a code of practice for BCM and incorporates the best practice from PAS 56, the BCM guidelines that support the UK Civil Contingencies Act 2004 and other sources from around the world. In 2007 BSI published Part 2 of the new standard that provides a Specification for BCM against which organizations may be certified. This book is designed to help organizations meet the Specification for BCM, BS 25999-2.

## Evolution of business continuity management

The concept of business continuity was developed in the mid-1980s as a new way of managing business risks. The basis of BCM is that it is the key responsibility of company directors to ensure the continuation of business functionality at all times and under any circumstances.

BCM grew out of requirements in the early 1970s to provide computer disaster recovery for information systems. Traditionally disaster planning had concentrated on the restoration of facilities after a major incident such as the loss of computing or telecommunications, or the loss of a building or plant through fire or flood. The responsibility for these plans had been dispersed to various functions within a company. Typically these were the IT, estates and security departments. Disaster recovery plans in general are written on the basis of recovery after an event.

Unexpected events do not simply happen; quite often they are created by the organization itself. Every organization has inherent weaknesses: faulty IT systems that are 'worked around', informal communication channels, lack of operator training, disconnects in structures and local process variations. Examination into the causes of most major disasters has found that there are several incidents or circumstances that combine together, leading to the eventual disaster.

BCM is about prevention, not just cure. It is not just about being able to deal with incidents as and when they occur and thus prevent a crisis and subsequent disaster, but also about establishing a culture within the organization that seeks to build greater resilience in order to ensure the continuity of product and service delivery to clients and customers.

> BCM establishes a strategic and operational framework to implement, proactively, an organization's resilience to disruption, interruption or loss in supplying its products and services. It should not purely be a reactive measure taken after an incident has occurred. BCM requires planning across many facets of an organization, therefore its resilience depends equally on its management and operational staff, as well as technology, and requires a holistic approach to be taken when establishing a BCM programme (PAS 56:2003).

Business continuity management is about anticipating that things are beginning to go wrong and taking planned and rehearsed steps to protect the business and hence the stakeholders' interests. It is about maintaining their confidence in the management's ability to handle a crisis and to prevent disasters occurring, thus protecting the brand, reputation and image of the organization as much as its physical infrastructure and employees. BCM goes beyond recovery from a disaster to establishing a culture that seeks to prevent failure and crisis.

Knight and Pretty of Templeton College, Oxford, undertook research in the mid-1990s that showed that the impact of disasters on shareholder value can be serious (Knight and Pretty, 2000). They discovered that it is the lack of confidence in the ability of senior managers and directors to act quickly and professionally at the time of disaster that drives down share values. Effective BCM integrates with crisis/incident management to ensure that if a major incident does occur then not only is the organization able to maintain continuity of operations, it is also able to reassure the stakeholder community that it is in control.

## The business drivers

Although it is widely accepted that the protection of brand, reputation and image is paramount for any organization, other, external drivers have greater influence over the introduction of business continuity management (see Figure 1.1).

Industry regulations and legal requirements are having an increasing impact in driving organizations to establish BCM. There is greater awareness among regulators that organizations should have effective BCM in place for the protection of customers and the community. Since the attack on the World Trade Centre in New York on 11 September 2001 finance regulators across the world have set out conditions for BCM that they expect the firms they regulate to follow. In some cases these conditions are mandatory; in others they provide strong guidance.

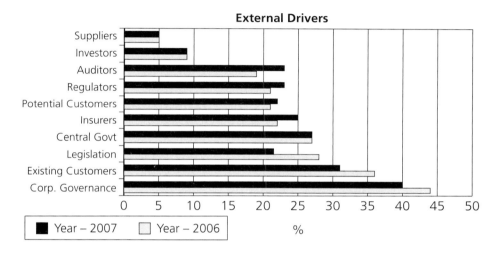

**Figure 1.1 – External drivers for BCM (source: Chartered Management Institute, 2007)**

In the UK the Civil Contingencies Act 2004 requires local government bodies, the National Health Service and emergency services to put in place effective BCM to ensure that they can continue to perform their functions in the event of an emergency. They have to ensure they can mobilize the functions they need to deal with the emergency, minimize the impact on the responder's day-to-day activity, and maintain vital services for the community at an appropriate level. In addition local authorities have the responsibility of promoting business continuity to business and appropriate voluntary bodies in support of the concept of a resilient community.

Insurance companies are having an increasing influence. Business interruption insurance is seen as a way of covering the revenue lost following a major disruption. Until relatively recently the insurance market linked business interruption insurance to building insurance. More recently they have sought to sever this link as business interruption losses have increased dramatically. Underwriters are looking for evidence that effective business continuity management is in place to reduce their risk exposure to business interruption.

One of the most significant drivers today is that of corporate governance. Across the world, regulation and legislation in this area is increasing. In the UK the revision of stock exchange listing rules places greater emphasis on internal controls to manage the principal risks facing a company.

When the Turnbull Committee's *Guidance for Directors* on internal controls was first published in September 1999 (Turnbull et al., 1999) the chair of the committee, Nigel Turnbull, stated, 'The Guidance sets out an overall framework of best practice for business, based upon an assessment and control of their significant risks. For many companies, business continuity management will address some of these key risks and help them to achieve compliance' (Nigel Turnbull, personal communication).

Another group acting as a key external driver are auditors, who look for evidence of effective BCM being in place to meet regulations and legislation. Previously they asked if business continuity plans existed. Their current approach is to look for evidence that the plan is rehearsed and that BCM has been promoted within the organization.

Motivated by these external drivers and the need to manage principal risks, organizations have identified that they are often dependent upon key suppliers for their own continuity. As a result the pressure for BCM has started to flow down the supply chain from customers. Just as major customers have insisted that their suppliers have quality and project management processes in place, they are now demanding that BCM be established to ensure continuity of supply. This is driven not only by their need to achieve regulatory compliance, but also by the need to maintain their market share. The need for better management across the supply network was highlighted by the UK fuel crisis of September 2000.

There are a number of factors that have emerged in the last decade or so that might be considered to have increased the level of risk in supply chains. These include: the adoption of 'lean' practices, the globalization of supply chains, focused factories and centralized distribution, the trend to outsourcing, reduction in the supplier base, volatility of demand and the lack of visibility and control procedures.

A breakdown of drivers by sector and company size is contained in Appendix A.

Future drivers may include investors and banks who would wish to see that continuity is built into business plans as well as public authorities and emergency services that are driven by the Civil Contingencies Act and will require their partners and suppliers to have effective BCM. Additional pressure may come from trade and professional bodies and the public in general via the media and pressure groups.

A local authority in the North West of England has identified that they fund voluntary organizations that provide a vital service, on the authority's behalf, to some of the most vulnerable in their community. They need to be certain that these organizations are able to continue, especially at the time of a major emergency affecting the area.

> The council department responsible for these services now requires that any organization receiving funding from the authority must have business continuity in place if the funding is to be maintained. The council offers help and advice to the voluntary organizations on the establishment of BCM.

Time has become a key driver for business continuity management. The speed of business has changed and there is very often little time to allow for a gradual recovery. The emergence of e-commerce and the lack of loyalty among customers have changed the need for recovery to one of availability. Organizations for which this is vital have to ensure that their services are available 24 hours a day, seven days a week, 365 days a year. Customers will not wait if a call centre is not answering or a website is not available.

It is the time dimension that has created the move to BCM and is the principal differentiator between risk management and continuity management. It is argued that business continuity should not be considered subordinate to risk management. There is a risk management function that sits within business continuity. There may also be a separate risk management activity outside of this function, but not above it, that deals with the day-to-day risk of conducting business. This will vary from organization to organization.

## Benefits of BCM

Implementing BCM can bring real benefits to an organization aside from meeting the requirements of regulators, customers and the law.

Competitive advantage can be gained for organizations that are able to demonstrate to potential customers that they have proven plans to continue supply in the face of disruption. Certification against or compliance with BS 25999-2 can be used as part of a marketing package to attract new customers as well as providing them with a positive reason to renew existing contracts.

Financial benefits will occur when areas of weakness within the organization are eliminated. Within processes, duplications and omissions exist that are wasteful in time and resources. Every failure that occurs has a cost to the organization, even if it does not result in a disruption. By eliminating these weaknesses the organization becomes more resilient and more cost-effective.

Further financial gain may occur if effective BCM exists as it can influence the approach taken by insurers to business interruption insurance. It can affect the level of cover offered, the amount of excess that is applied to a policy or reduce the premiums levied.

One of the greatest threats to an organization during a disruption is the interruption to cash flow. In enabling the continued delivery of key products and services, effective BCM contributes to the maintenance of cash flow. For many organizations this can be critical as they are dependent on their ability to maintain operations in order to service debt.

A printer ran a successful one-man business in a small UK town. He was reasonably priced and relatively quick. Five weeks before Christmas he had a problem with his press and could not print orders. He did not inform his customers of the difficulties but waited for them to contact him. He had no maintenance contract on his press and when he did get an engineer to the site he was advised that it was a machine for which there were no spares in stock and they would have to come from Japan.

It was three weeks before he was back in production. Many of his customers had gone elsewhere as they needed their printing completed before Christmas. Being based in a small town his failing was soon known and his reputation suffered as a result. The following March he wrote to all his existing customers advising them that he was no longer able to continue to service their needs as the company was closing due to lack of business.

There are some vital lessons for small companies to be taken from this case. If you have a single machine on which you rely, ensure you have a maintenance contract in place with a company who services that model. Make arrangements with a similar company outside the area whereby you both undertake to meet the other company's orders in the event of being disrupted – mutual aid. And finally, if you have a problem then advise your customers and explain what you are doing to meet their requirements.

If correctly introduced, BCM encourages greater staff involvement in the successful running of the organization. By listening to the people who actually do the job it is possible to eliminate many of the lower level risks that can disrupt an organization. It is often the front line staff that can identify where weaknesses and single points of failure exist and how to improve processes and resilience. These staff will welcome an opportunity to contribute and a chance for their ideas and concerns to be acknowledged and, if appropriate, implemented.

Every organization has a duty of care to its employees, customers, clients, the community and the environment. BCM can be seen as part of a social responsibility agenda, helping to discharge these duties and maintaining employment throughout the period of disruption.

The most valuable asset of any organization – public, private or voluntary – is its reputation; it can take years to build up and moments to destroy. Elements of BCM are designed to ensure that every effort is made to protect brand reputation and image throughout and beyond a period of disruption.

## Why adopt BS 25999?

As BCM has developed worldwide, there has been a convergence in the methodologies being promoted. It became apparent following the Year 2000 problem or 'millennium bug', when organizations were deluged with requests for compliance statements from their customers and clients, that there was a need for a uniform approach to BCM.

It is undesirable for major customers to enforce their own approach to BCM down their supply chains, as happened with other management systems, notably quality. While a supplier can run different quality systems to meet the requirements of its customer base, it cannot run different, and possibly conflicting, BCM systems, which will be used during a disruption at a time when tensions are high. This was one of the principal drivers for establishing a Standard for BCM.

BS 25999 was created to set out a uniform benchmark in good practice, satisfying the needs of customers, clients, government, regulators and all other interested parties.

By adopting the standard approach to BCM as set out in BS 25999, organizations can offer their customers and clients greater assurance that they will be capable of managing continuity at the time of disruption.

# 2. Implementing BS 25999

The British Standard for business continuity management consists of two parts:

- BS 25999-1, *Business continuity management. Part 1 – Code of practice*. This document takes the form of good practice guidance and recommendations, indicating what practices an organization should or may undertake to implement effective BCM. Organizations may choose to follow all or part of the Code of practice. The Code can be used for self-assessment or between organizations. The Code is not a specification for BCM.
- BS 25999-2, *Business continuity management – Part 2: Specification*. This document sets out specifically what an organization shall do to implement BCM. It is for use by internal and external parties, including certification bodies, to assess the organization's ability to meet regulatory and customer requirements as well as the organization's own requirements. BS 25999-2 contains only those requirements that can be objectively audited and a demonstration of successful implementation can therefore be used by an organization to assure interested parties that an appropriate business continuity management system (BCMS) is in place.

In common with modern management system standards, BS 25999-2 utilizes the PDCA (Plan-Do-Check-Act) cycle for developing, implementing and improving the effectiveness of an organization's business continuity management system.

## Management Systems Approach – PDCA

The Plan-Do-Check-Act methodology is based upon the work of Walter Shewhart who developed statistical process control in the US during the 1930s. It was taken up and promoted very effectively from the 1950s and onwards by the famous quality management authority, W. Edwards Deming, and is used extensively to achieve continual improvement in management systems. Figure 2.1 shows the Shewhart or Deming cycle.

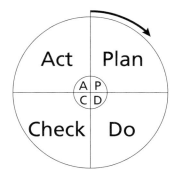

**Figure 2.1 – The Shewhart or Deming cycle**

Figure 2.2 shows how the PDCA cycle is applied to the BCMS as set out in BS 25999-2. The PDCA model produces business continuity outcomes that meet the requirements and expectations of interested parties.

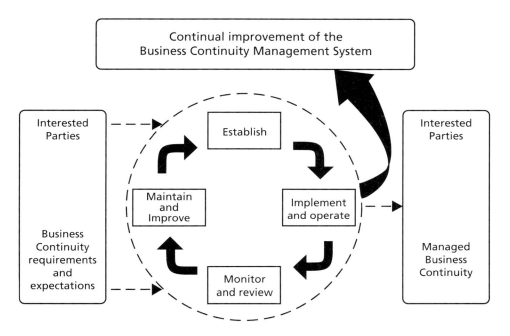

**Figure 2.2 – Plan, Do, Check, Act cycle (source: BS 25999-2:2007)**

The elements of the PDCA cycle as it relates to BCM, as set out in BS 25999-2, are as follows.

## Plan

Establish business continuity policy, objectives, targets, controls, processes and procedures relevant to managing risk and improving business continuity to deliver results in accordance with an organization's overall policies and objectives.

## Do

Implement and operate the business continuity policy, controls, processes and procedures.

## Check

Monitor and review performance against business continuity policy, objectives and practical experience, and report the results to management for review, and determine and authorize actions for remediation and improvement.

## Act

Maintain and improve the BCMS by taking corrective and preventive actions, based on the results of management review and reappraising the scope of the BCMS and business continuity policy and objectives.

The PDCA approach as used in BS 25999-2 ensures there is a degree of consistency with other management system standards, such as BS EN ISO 9001:2000 (Quality Management Systems) and BS EN ISO 14001:2004 (Environmental Management Systems).

## The BCM life cycle

Initial work by practitioners in 1999 resulted in a widely accepted representation of the BCM life cycle. With the publication of BS 25999-1 in 2006, a new illustration of the BCM life cycle was introduced (see Figure 2.3).

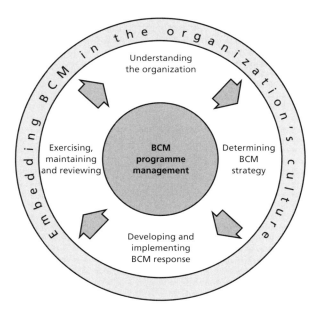

**Figure 2.3 – The BCM life cycle (source: BS 25999-1:2006)**

It is accepted that the PDCA approach can be applied to every element of the BCM life cycle but, for the purposes of this publication, the following approach has been taken.

Figure 2.3 could be described as the BCM wheel. The hub (BCM programme management) and the tyre (Embedding BCM in the organization's culture) are the elements that relate to Plan, Check and Act in the PDCA cycle. The spokes (Understanding the organization, Determining BCM strategy, Developing and implementing BCM response and Exercising, maintaining and reviewing) represent the Do element of the cycle.

The rest of this book describes approaches that will enable those responsible for BCM in an organization, regardless of size or sector, to meet the requirements of BS 25999-2.

# 3. Planning the business continuity management system

Chapters 3–6 address the Plan element of the PDCA cycle as set out in BS 25999-2.

To be successful a BCMS must be introduced and supported by the top management of the organization. Their involvement is required from the outset and their ongoing support is essential if BCM is to be taken seriously by the organization as a whole.

It is important that as the process is developed and embedded in the organization, evidence of decisions, activities, planning, etc. are assembled and retained for any subsequent audits required for compliance assessment or certification against BS 25999-2.

## The first steps

At the heart of the BCM life cycle is programme management. It was given this title rather than project management because a project has a beginning and end but BCM has to be seen as a continuous process. It should be considered as a programme of projects designed to ensure a current, relevant and assured business continuity management system exists within an organization.

In establishing and managing the BCMS, the organization is required to establish:

- the requirements for business continuity, taking into account the organization's objectives and obligations as well as regulatory, contractual and legal duties;
- interests of key stakeholders;
- the scope of business continuity in terms of its key products and services.

## Determining the BCM requirements

The first stage is to be clear as to why the organization is introducing BCM. Is it seen as a good thing to have because it will make the organization more resilient, profitable or competitive? Is it recognized that BCM is an important element in managing risk to ensure the organization achieves its goals? Is it because others have done it, so will we?

Are there other pressures driving the introduction of business continuity? Is it because of the external drivers that were highlighted in Chapter 1?

A good place to start is to understand the environment in which the organization operates. Various analytical tools are available to assist this, one of which is STEEPLE (see Figure 3.1), which focuses on external environments.

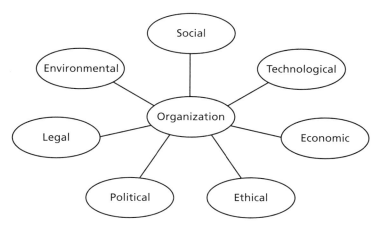

**Figure 3.1 – STEEPLE analysis**

Some of the questions that have to be answered for each element of the analysis are:

- What are the social responsibilities the organization has to the community, e.g. employment, safety? How does society view the activities of the organization, e.g. as a threat, with suspicion?
- How dependent is the organization upon external technologies, e.g. communications? How does the rapid advance in technology impact the organization?
- What is the economic climate in which the organization operates? What is the attitude towards debt by the financial institutions the organization is involved with? How strong are the economies of the countries in which and with whom the organization trades?
- What are the ethics of trade? What is the perception of the public and the media towards the organization and its activities?
- What is the political climate in which the organization operates? Would a change of government affect attitudes towards the organization and its sector? What are the chances of terrorism and civil unrest affecting the organization?
- Which laws and regulations apply? Are they national or international?
- And finally, what environmental considerations does the organization have to take account of? What is the organization's own impact on the environment, e.g. pollution? What are the external events that could impact the organization, e.g. from nature or from neighbours?

> On Sunday 11 December 2005 a major explosion occurred at the Buncefield oil depot on the edge of Hemel Hempstead in the UK. There was no loss of life but the subsequent fire was the largest to occur in peacetime Europe and caused significant property damage and disruption to businesses adjacent to the site.

630 businesses employing 16,500 people were disrupted for two days. 88 of these businesses were severely impacted. Many buildings and their contents were completely destroyed, access to many other premises and their stock was denied for many days. Some businesses relocated away from Hemel Hempstead, placing pressure on employees forced to travel long distances to work.

The lesson to be learnt from Buncefield is that it is essential to assess the risks that your neighbours pose to you and the environment.

Understanding clearly why BCM is being introduced and how quickly this has to be done is vital because this will influence the scope and depth of the first pass around the BCM life cycle.

## Establishing the business continuity objectives and plans

Once the reasons for introducing BCM have been agreed by the organization's top management the objectives and plans for the introduction of the BCMS can be set out. The use of project management tools and techniques is recommended with implementation plans set as Pert or Gantt charts. These can be subsequently submitted as evidence if the BCMS is subject to audit.

If the organization is dependent upon key suppliers, intermediaries or partners for the delivery of key products and services to its customers/clients then it is essential that any introduction of BCM acknowledges this and the BCM objectives and plans reflect the need to ensure the effectiveness of the key suppliers' or partners' BCM arrangements.

## Scoping BCM

Determining what will be covered by the business continuity management system is critical. The first question a certification body will ask of an organization being audited against BS 25999-2 relates to the scope. More importantly, external bodies interested in the organization's BCM capabilities will want to know what is covered by the process.

Factors that influence the scope are:

• the size and complexity of the organization;
• the needs of customers, clients, regulators, auditors, insurers and investors;
• the type of activity undertaken by the organization;
• the environment and location in which it operates;
• the organization's objectives.

A large and complex body is unlikely to introduce a BCMS for the entire organization at the initial pass but rather commence with the products and services that are critical to meeting the objectives of the organization and the requirements of the external stakeholders. A small organization is better able to encompass all of its activities first time round.

Whatever the decision, it is vital that the scope of the BCMS is defined and documented at the outset of the programme. An example of a scoping document can be found in Appendix B. It is possible to include the scope within the policy document. However, if the scope changes, the policy document will also require updating.

## Setting the business continuity policy

The creation and publication of the organization's BCM policy document, signed by an executive director, is a key element of the BCMS and a clear demonstration of the organization's commitment.

The policy document should set out:

• the objectives for the establishment and maintenance of BCM within the organization;
• the scope of business continuity, including limitations and exclusions;
• an overview of the roles and responsibilities of those charged with delivering BCM;
• the resources allocated to BCM;
• the BCM principles, guidelines and standards that will apply;
• a reference to any legal or regulatory requirements;
• the basis on which the BCMS will be measured and reviewed.

The final point relates to how the organization assures itself that the BCMS is being correctly implemented and maintained within the organization. One way this can be done is by the setting of KPIs (key performance indicators) that are used by management to monitor the BCMS. Examples of KPIs are:

• the number of plans to be completed by a specified date;
• the number of awareness sessions to be completed by a specified date;
• the number of plans to be exercised, and types of exercise carried out, by a specified date;
• lessons learned from these exercises to be implemented within a specified timescale;
• the percentage of plans to be reviewed by annual review date;
• the level of impact caused by disruptive incidents in a 12-month period.

The policy document should be brief and appropriate to the organization, taking into consideration the nature, scale, complexity, geography and criticality of its activities. It must also reflect the culture, dependencies and operating environment. If there is a standard format for policy documents in the organization then this should be followed.

The BCM policy document, once approved and signed off by top management, should be published within the organization and may be made available to appropriate stakeholders. Key public sector bodies covered by the UK Contingencies Act 2004 are required to make their BCM policy documents publicly available. These may be published on their websites or be available on request. There may be commercial advantage for private companies in similarly publishing their BCM policy documents. Listed companies could include reference to their policy in the annual reports and accounts, providing assurance to investors and other interested parties that they take business continuity seriously.

The BCM policy, like all other policies within the organization, should be subject to regular review at an interval appropriate to the organization or when significant changes occur to the organization or the environment in which it operates. A sample policy document is included in Appendix C.

# 4. Resourcing BCM

## Financing the programme

If the introduction and ongoing maintenance of BCM is to be successful then sufficient resources must be allocated to the programme. Top management frequently view BCM as a 'grudge purchase' and they require a return on investment (ROI) to be demonstrated. This can be difficult as BCM is designed to maintain continuity in the unlikely event of a disruptive incident occurring.

The arguments for BCM are based more on economics than accountancy. It is the opportunity cost of failure that has to be weighed against the investments required. Examples of opportunity costs are:

- the cost to the organization, in lost sales, if production is disrupted for more than 'X' hours;
- the financial penalties that will be incurred if the service/product cannot be delivered;
- the value placed on lost customers if disruptions last more than 'X' days (taking into account that to win new customers is very expensive);
- the value of lost contracts, or the inability to win new ones, as a result of being excluded for not having a BCMS in place.

The level of resource required to implement and maintain a BCMS is appropriate to the size and nature of the organization and the environment in which it operates. For smaller organizations BCM does not have to be complex and appropriate BCM can be established at minimal cost. What is important is that sufficient time is allocated to those who are tasked with implementing the BCM programme. Once established, BCM should become part of normal business practice.

## Roles and responsibilities

Executive management sits at the heart of effective business continuity management regardless of company size. All new management processes introduced to organizations require champions at a high level. This may be the managing director of a small company, a director of a major PLC or an executive within a local authority who can take authority over and accountability for BCM and can demonstrate ongoing support for the initiative. A clear demonstration of this high-level commitment must be made across the organization at the very outset and must always be maintained.

An appropriate structure should be established that suits the organization.

A small organization may have a senior manager who has responsibility for the introduction and management of the BCM system. International businesses frequently have large teams that work throughout the world to establish and maintain BCM across the organization.

The level of BCM resources at the centre of the organization should be kept to the minimum and be appropriate to the size and geographical spread of the organization. BCM must be owned by the organization at the operational level. Creating a BCM department will enforce a 'silo' culture and undermine the inclusive principle that should be established through the belief that continuity is part of everyone's job. Figure 4.1 sets out a structure for a medium-sized organization. The BCM structures used within the organization must be clearly documented.

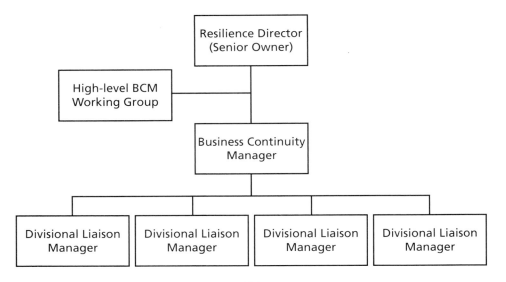

**Figure 4.1 – Possible BCM structure**

A high-level working group should be drawn from the senior management at division, product and/or service level. The role of the group is:

- to take overall control of resource allocation;
- to set priorities for the organization;
- to interpret the board's attitude towards risk;
- to set continuity strategies in line with the organization's objectives and responsibilities;
- to establish the measures that will be used to assure the BCM process remains current and relevant.

This group is also responsible for ensuring that the importance of BCM is communicated throughout the organization and that stakeholders are kept informed. The approach the high-level working group takes will have a strong influence on the culture within the organization. In a small organization this role may fall to the owner or managing director, who may be assisted by a senior employee.

In a larger organization, divisional liaison managers are responsible for the introduction and maintenance of the BCM process within their area of operation. Very often these individuals have BCM added to their existing roles and responsibilities rather than being solely dedicated to the process.

Organizations that have successfully introduced BCM have used a 'matrix' management approach: a team of managers who understand the business and are able to appreciate how the functions operate and resources are utilized. Such teams may have representatives from the executive, operational management, legal, finance, technology (ICT), facilities, purchasing, security, HR, suppliers, etc. Their role is to advise the high-level working group throughout the BCM process.

## Training and competency

Assigning roles and responsibilities is not enough. The organization must ensure that all personnel who are assigned business continuity roles and responsibilities are competent to perform the required tasks. The tasks may be in BCM development and planning or in an actual invocation following a major disruption. Under these circumstances people need to know what is expected of them and they must have the capabilities to perform the required tasks, often under stress. This is an area that can get overlooked. One major government department found that there were people named in its business continuity plans who did not know they were included.

BCM training is a key element of BS 25999-2 and is a statutory requirement placed on local government, emergency services and the NHS under the UK Civil Contingencies Act 2004. Financial resources must be set aside for this activity.

There are some key steps to be taken to ensure appropriate levels of BCM training and competencies exist within the organization:

- determining the necessary competencies for those who will work on BCMS (Appendix D contains a sample list of competencies for a BCM team);
- conducting training needs analysis on staff being assigned BCM roles and responsibilities in the development of the BCMS and those who will be involved when a plan is invoked;
- providing the training;
- evaluating the effectiveness of the training provided;
- maintaining records of education, training skills, experience and qualifications.

Appendix E sets out a process for establishing a training programme.

---

# 5. Embedding BCM in the organization's culture

The outer part of the BCM life cycle relates to an organization's culture. To be successful, business continuity has to become part of the way that an organization is managed, regardless of size or sector. At each stage of the BCM process opportunities exist to introduce and enhance an organization's BCM culture.

BS 25999-2 requires the organization to:

- ensure all personnel are aware of how they contribute to the achievement of the organization's business continuity objectives;
- raise, enhance and maintain awareness by establishing an ongoing BCM education and information programme for all staff;
- introduce a process for evaluating the effectiveness of BCM awareness delivery.

Building, promoting and embedding a BCM culture within an organization ensures that it becomes part of the organization's core values and effective management.

An organization with a positive BCM culture will benefit, as it will:

- develop a BCM programme more efficiently;
- instil confidence in its stakeholders, especially staff and customers, in its ability to handle business disruptions;
- increase its resilience over time by ensuring BCM implications are considered in decisions at all levels for existing products and services as well as for new ones;
- minimize the likelihood and impact of disruptions.

Creating and embedding a BCM culture within an organization can be a lengthy and difficult process that might encounter a level of resistance that was not anticipated. An understanding of the existing culture within the organization will assist in the development of an appropriate BCM culture programme.

To be effective, BCM must not be seen as a 'bolt-on' or as a 'passing initiative' from senior management. Before the process can start, the board or executive team has to accept the importance and value of the BCM process. They need to encourage a management approach that contemplates the 'what ifs' or considers what might prevent delivery of the organization's products/services.

To be successful, BCM must be 'owned' by everyone within an organization.

Many disruptions are caused by internal failures. Within many organizations there exists a blame culture that prevents people from flagging up problems. If the culture is about only wanting to hear the 'good news' then there will be a reluctance to draw attention to failings, which may subsequently lead to disruptions.

All staff, including middle management, must be convinced that business continuity management is a serious issue for the organization and that they have an important role to play in maintaining the delivery of products and services to their clients and customers. It is essential that awareness programmes are established as part of the overall introduction of BCM.

Raising awareness is done in two stages. The first is to ensure that all those in the organization are aware BCM is being introduced and why. They will need to be convinced that this is a lasting initiative that has the support of the executive.

A technique which was used very successfully in the introduction of total quality management in the 1980s was to hold team meetings at each level of the organization to introduce the concept and to ask the team to consider how it could improve the quality of its output. The same principle can be applied to BCM, with the teams being asked to identify aspects that prevent or impede the continuity of their areas of operation. The key questions to ask such a group are the 'what ifs' since this style of question gets the group thinking about its contribution to continuity. Experience has shown that even at the lowest level, employees are able to relate to the BCM concept and not only identify areas of potential disconnect but also possible solutions that can maintain continuity.

Each organization will have a level of management that is particularly sceptical about the introduction of new initiatives; this is very often middle management. Particular emphasis must be given to gaining its support if BCM is to become part of the organization's culture. This management level will also have a large part to play in the initial charting of critical activities and processes, so gaining its support at an early stage is vital.

The second stage of raising awareness occurs once the business continuity plans (BCPs) have been produced. It is important that all stakeholders are aware that the organization has such plans in place. This will help to raise their level of confidence in the organization's ability to deal with disruptions.

Employees need to have confidence that their jobs will be protected while the disruption is being contained. It is also critical that individuals know what actions they are required to take when the plan is invoked.

---

A major UK retailer has a communications policy that is designed to ensure its employees know what to do if an incident occurs. They are given a number to call if they become aware of an incident at work or they see a news report, etc. concerning a disruption at their work location. When one of their London stores caught fire the employees knew what to do the next day. Some went to previously designated alternative locations; others remained at home and called the staff help line for recorded advice.

Lesson: ensure employees are kept informed about what is needed from them at the time of disruption.

---

Employees new to an organization must be made aware of the BCM policy and their part in the business continuity plans. This can be accomplished by incorporating BCM material into the staff induction programme. Awareness of the overall BCM programme can be maintained by using internal newspapers, emails, the organization's intranet, team meetings and broadcasts from senior management. These may highlight examples where the organization successfully managed an incident, praising those involved. It may also draw upon lessons learned from the failures of other organizations.

One major UK telecommunications company has included an element of continuity in management objectives and has a comprehensive online training programme that all managers must undertake. A major London Borough has gone one step further and linked BCM objectives to performance-related pay.

A forward-looking organization should include continuity in its mission/vision statement, e.g. 'to continue to be the most successful supplier of ....' If the management's key objectives flow from the mission statement then they should also include continuity.

The purchasing department in the organization has an important role to play in ensuring that key suppliers are made aware of the importance of BCM to the organization and the processes they should adopt to ensure continuity of supply. This applies to existing and new supply contracts.

Those responsible for new product development should be encouraged to build continuity solutions into the design of the product and its supporting processes. It is easier and more cost-effective to design-in continuity at the concept stage than to add it as a 'bolt on' after a problem has arisen. One Australian bank will not allow a product to be launched onto the market unless an appropriate continuity solution has been incorporated.

All staff have to understand that BCM is a serious issue for the organization and that they have an important role to play in maintaining the delivery of products and services to their clients and customers.

Raising awareness does not stop with the internal stakeholders. Those outside the organization must also be made aware of the actions that will be taken at the time of any disruption.

Customers will need to know how their supply of goods and services will be affected and when they can expect a return to normal working. Suppliers will need to know the alternative locations they are required to deliver supplies to and also need to be confident that they will be paid. The banks and investors will need to have confidence in the management being able to handle the disruption effectively and need to know their investments are safe.

Regulators, legislators and others with statutory responsibilities will need to understand the alternative arrangements that are in place to meet the organization's statutory and regulatory requirements. The wider community may need to be informed of actions that would be taken if the disruption could have a serious impact on their welfare, e.g. a chemical plant fire.

# 6. Documentation and records

## Document control

A key element of any management system is the control and management of documentation. With BCM this is critical since at the time of any disruption it is essential that all players have access to and work from authorized and current incident or continuity plans and supporting documentation. Much of the information contained within the BCMS documentation will be of a sensitive nature and therefore must be subject to appropriate protection and confidentiality markings.

The management of the organization must therefore establish and maintain a documented and controlled system of records management that covers identification, storage, protection, retrieval, retention time and disposal of documents and records.

## Documentation required

The organization must have documentation covering the following aspects of the BCMS:

* the business continuity management policy;
* the scope of the BCMS;
* the procedures and controls in support of the BCMS;
* the results of the business impact analysis and risk assessments;
* the BCM strategy;
* business continuity and incident management plans;
* up-to-date contact and mobilization details for personnel and any relevant agencies, organizations and resources that might be required to support the response strategies;
* an exercise schedule, results and corrective and preventative actions;
* post-incident reviews;
* a training programme.

Any organization that is subject to audit, either voluntarily or as a result of a mandatory requirement, will be required to provide documentary evidence relating to their BCMS. The above list provides a useful guide to appropriate documentation. Those wishing to be certified to BS 25999-2 will have to adhere to this list as a minimum.

## Records management

Proving that a BCM system is effective is one of the key challenges facing any organization. Records should be kept of the management of the BCMS and of exercises, incidents, outcomes and lessons learned.

Evidence from such records can be used to demonstrate to internal management that the policy is adhered to and objectives are being met. The outcomes and lessons learned from exercises and incidents will help to justify the investment made in BCM to the top management of the organization.

External stakeholders will also be interested in such records. In the event of an inquiry or legal claim being mounted against an organization that has experienced a major incident and failed to maintain the supply of critical products/services, evidence will be required of how the BCMS and the incident was managed. Being unable to produce such evidence may harm the organization.

Chapters 3–6 covered the Plan element of the business continuity management system, incorporating the policy, structure, resources, training and assurance, as set out in the hub (programme management) and the tyre (culture) of the BCM life cycle, shown in Figure 2.3. Chapter 7 looks at the Do element of the PDCA cycle.

# 7. Developing BCM

This section covers the Do element of the PDCA cycle and considers the spokes of the wheel of the BCM life cycle (see Figure 2.3). These include:

* understanding the organization;
* determining business continuity strategy;
* developing and implementing a BCM response;
* exercising, maintaining and reviewing.

Many organizations start by developing continuity plans against perceived risks such as loss of IT or a building. This is the traditional disaster recovery approach, which delivers a degree of comfort to senior managers in that something has been done to protect the organization. However, it has an inherent problem in that it might overlook critical activities outside of these facilities and services and not meet the actual needs of the business.

The direction that BCM has now taken is based on ensuring the continuity of critical activities and processes that deliver key products/services to clients and customers. This is more aligned with total quality management, which is based on supplier/customer relationships and the processes that serve them.

Every organization has inputs and outputs regardless of size, sector or type, e.g. a commercial business, public body, voluntary organization or charity. All have customers or clients to whom they deliver products or services. The drivers for the organization to deliver these products and services may be different, e.g. profit, community service, legislation or regulation. They will vary from sector to sector and are dependent on the size of the organization. In addition there are many stakeholders who have a keen interest in what the organization delivers and how the products and services are produced.

## Understanding the organization

### Stakeholder identification

All stakeholders must be identified at the start. This enables the organization to consider continuity solutions against stakeholder requirements and perceptions. Some stakeholders are obvious: shareholders, customers, clients, employees and suppliers. Additional stakeholders include regulators, financial investors (banks), insurance companies, auditors, professional bodies, trade associations and government departments. Some are less obvious: competitors, the community (both permanent and transitory), the environment in which the organization operates, the media and protest groups. The latter two can have considerable influence on the public's perception of the organization.

Shell attempted to sink the redundant Brent Spa oil platform in the North Sea in June 1995 following research into the best method of disposal and the granting of a disposal licence by the UK government. Shell was not prepared for the actions of the protest group Greenpeace, who objected to the sinking on the grounds that the marine environment would be polluted by the structure's contents.

Although Shell tried to publicly counter Greenpeace's arguments, the protest group provided the majority of the material for the world's media and hence won the support of the public and subsequently that of the German government. Shell was forced to abandon the sinking and the platform was eventually broken up on land.

Shell UK had been warned by their German operation that there would be considerable protest activity to prevent the sinking but, having secured a UK government licence, felt it could ignore Greenpeace. Shell's reputation was damaged as a result.

A simple technique that can be used to identify stakeholders and their expectations, both under normal and disrupted conditions, is to assemble a group of senior managers and get them to list the stakeholders and their expectations and then to rank the stakeholders in order of importance for the organization. The exercise has the additional benefit of helping the management team to look at the organization from the stakeholders' point of view rather than from within. Particular emphasis should be placed on the expectations of the customers and clients of the organization.

A template for a stakeholder analysis is included in Appendix F.

## Business impact analysis (BIA)

The next stage is to define the critical activities that enable the organization to fulfil its mission/vision and high-level objectives. It is essential to identify the key products or services that, if disrupted for any reason, would have the greatest impact upon the organization and its stakeholders. It is these products or services on which BCM must be concentrated initially. Once BCM has been successfully established to deal with these key products or services there will be the opportunity to extend BCM to other areas of the organization.

In analysing the way products or services are delivered an approach must be taken that breaks with the traditional functional view of the organization. A large multinational IT services company uses a methodology that considers what activities are involved to get from 'quote to cash'. That is to say, what is needed to get into a position to quote against a tender, win the business, deliver to the customer's satisfaction and then invoice for the goods and to receive payment. It requires an 'end-to-end' view of the organization and its activities.

Consideration must also be given to any third party's role in these activities. Third parties include suppliers, outsourcers and intermediaries (see Figure 7.1).

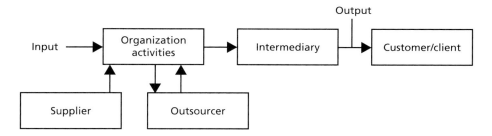

**Figure 7.1 – The end-to-end view of delivery**

As their contract is with the organization, customers or clients will expect the organization to deliver the product or service regardless of the ability of the other players to maintain their continuity of operations. They will hold the organization responsible for failure.

As an example consider home care for the elderly. Local authorities are increasingly using third parties to deliver this service. However, if the service fails or is below standard it will not be the third-party intermediary that the client or their relatives will hold responsible but the local authority in whose name the service is being delivered. It is therefore essential that the local authority ensures the intermediary has effective BCM in place.

Michael Porter's value chain analysis (Porter, 1998) provides a useful methodology to assist in the understanding of how an organization works. The activities are broken down to ascertain where value is added. This provides a starting point in understanding how the organization works. Many senior managers make the assumption that they 'know how it works around here'. This is often not the case as the investigation into many disasters has clearly shown. If it is not understood how the organization works 'normally' then there is little chance of keeping it running at a time of a crisis.

## Impact versus risk

The traditional risk management approach would now consider what the threats/risks that could disrupt the critical activities that support key products or services and what could done to prevent them. Business continuity management on the other hand adopts an approach based on impact and time. It looks at the impact on the organization if critical activities are interrupted; it looks at effects rather than causes. While we can predict many threats, recent occurrences have shown that the unexpected can always happen, e.g. fuel shortages, foot and mouth disease,11 September 2001 in the US, the floods of 2007 and the loss of water supplies that resulted from them.

As stated before, BCM requires the organization to consider what the impact would be on itself and its stakeholders if the delivery of key products or services and their supporting critical activities were disrupted for any reason. This process is known as business impact analysis (BIA).

Measures of impact could be:

- financial loss;
- the impact on service delivery;
- embarrassment or loss of reputation;
- threat to personal safety;
- personal privacy infringement;
- failure to meet statutory or regulatory obligations;
- effect on project objectives and schedules.

The measures chosen must be appropriate; those for a commercial organization may be different from those for a public body.

The measures must also take into consideration time: how soon will the impact of the disruption to key products or services impinge upon the organization? How long before the organization is seriously affected by any disruption? In BS 25999-1 the term maximum tolerable period of disruption is used. This is defined as: 'the duration after which an organization's viability will be irrevocably threatened if product or service delivery cannot be resumed'.

For public sector organizations viability may be interpreted as loss of reputation.

Another measure of time must also be applied. Some products or services and their supporting activities are more critical at certain points in the calendar, e.g. key reporting dates, elections, payment dates (including payroll), school admissions, events associated with festivals, gritting of roads. In addition there may be key projects that have to be delivered on time and, if disrupted, will have serious consequences for the organization. As we cannot predict when any disruption will occur it is essential to chart these activities/events against a calendar (see Figure 7.2).

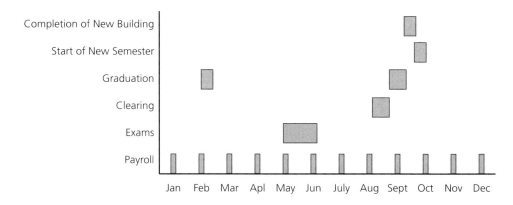

**Figure 7.2 – Key annual events for a university**

Consideration must also be given to disruptions and crises that occur outside the organization. The UK fuel shortage was an external event for most organizations but the impact was felt within.

> The 2005 product recall of over 600 food lines from UK shops containing Worcester Sauce contaminated with Sudan 1 (a carcinogenic food colouring), affected sales of Lea & Perrins Worcestershire Sauce despite this product containing no artificial colouring. Name association by the media and the public resulted in depressed demand for the Lea & Perrins product. 3500 customers called the Lea & Perrins help line in four days and the company had to launch an advertising campaign to protect the brand and its 90 per cent market share.
>
> Lesson: it might not be your failure that threatens your organization. Stakeholders' perceptions must be taken into account when undertaking BCM.

There are two ways to undertake business impact analysis. The first involves seeking input from operational management on what they consider critical to the organization. The results are collated and an attempt is made to rank the activities in order of priority for resumption. The danger in taking this approach is that many operational managers see their own areas of operation as critical and ranking will be difficult. It is also possible that when the analysis is presented to top management they may disagree on the findings.

The second approach is to use the senior management team – this may be the BCM high-level working group – to consider the organization as a whole and to provide a ranking for key products or services and the point at which MTPD (maximum tolerable period of disruption) occurs. This team will also need to set the timescale for resumption within the MTPD. This is called the RTO (recovery time objective) and it specifies the minimum levels at which key products or services must be resumed and the point in time by when full resumption must be achieved. The output is then used to determine the critical activities across the organization that are needed to deliver these products and services. This approach provides the quickest route to establishing the first round of BCM implementation.

A complex organization may have many products and services and, while all are important, some are more critical than others. For example, one UK county council delivers 170 services to the community. Following the BIA (business impact analysis) process it was established that 37 of these activities were key or vital for the community. With this knowledge the council concentrated their BCM activities on the most important areas for the authority and the community.

Appendix G provides a template for this stage of the BIA.

## Process mapping

Having gained the agreement of the high-level working group or senior management as to which are the key products or services, the next key stage is to identify the critical activities that support these products and services.

Processes, some formal, some informal, that have been established over time will support these critical activities. They all draw upon the resources of the organization and of third parties. The next stage is to identify these processes and the resources they use.

Process mapping should now be undertaken on the critical activities. The benefit of using this technique is that it will identify what actually happens in the organization in order to deliver the key products or services. The most dangerous step to take at this stage is for managers to assume they know how things are done in the organization. As managers rise through the organization they lose touch with practices on the ground. It is vital that we understand what actually happens in order to replicate this at the time of any disruption in order to provide a seamless continuity of operations.

It is possible that this has already been carried out in the organization. If so, the outputs should be examined to see if they are still current and relevant to BCM.

As an example consider the Acme Organization Ltd that delivers a range of facility management services. It has four main customer-facing divisions: Home Service, Estate Management, Domestic Installations and Commercial Contracts. These are supported by internal departments, one of which is purchasing, which also run the stores facilities for spares and equipment (see Figure 7.3).

The top management consider emergency call-out to be a key service for the home-based customer, as this is a contracted service to the local housing associations. The critical activities, supporting processes and resources now need to be identified together with any internal or external dependencies. This has to be done on an end-to-end basis for the whole service, from reception of call through to resolution, as this is what the customer expects from the organization.

The mapping starts with the high-level processes, e.g. dealing with a domestic customer's faulty heating system (see Figure 7.4).

The next level down is then mapped (see Figure 7.5).

There may be further levels of processes below these that also need to be recorded. The system used to record the processes may be paper-based or an appropriate software package.

The individuals who operate the processes should be involved in helping to map the way they work and the resources they use. Because people work in different ways and informal processes develop over time it is useful, where possible, to work with several people who are involved in operating the same process.

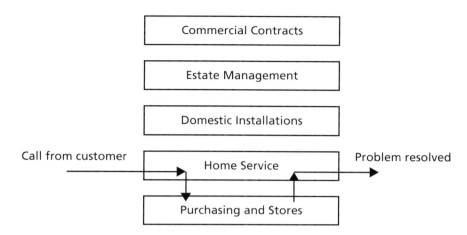

Figure 7.3 – Handling a home emergency call-out

Figure 7.4 – High-level process mapping example

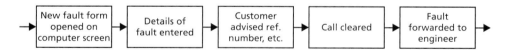

Figure 7.5 – Detailed process mapping example

The process mapping exercise opens up an opportunity for those delivering the service to raise areas where they experience difficulties – perhaps through the lack of resources, failure of supply, or breakdown in systems and security. They should also be asked about how they currently overcome disruptions to the process. Input at this level can identify continuity solutions that already exist but may not be documented and also areas where the organization can be made more resilient by reducing vulnerabilities.

## A process mapping tool

One simple form of process mapping is based on the use of adhesive notes. The person who operates the process is interviewed on what they do. The interviewer writes each stage of the process on a separate adhesive note, which is then attached to a flip chart (see Figure 7.6). The use of adhesive notes allows missed steps to be added without having to redraw the flow diagram. Very often those being interviewed will miss out steps as they assume the interviewer knows what happens next.

The next stage is to use different-coloured adhesive notes to chart resources used against steps in the process. The key resources used to support the processes may be people, information systems (ICT), facilities and suppliers. The numbers, location, skills, roles and responsibilities of the people required should be noted. The systems that support them must be logged, e.g. computer hardware, software applications, telecommunications and information (data). It should be noted what facilities in terms of premises, plant, machinery and materials are required. Very often third parties have a major role to play in critical activities as suppliers of goods and services, as outsourcers or as agents between the organization and its customers or clients. Their part in the process must be recorded.

As it is so important to the operation of any process it is recommended that a separate line and colour of adhesive note is used for information sources. When the mapping exercise is complete the output should be permanently recorded.

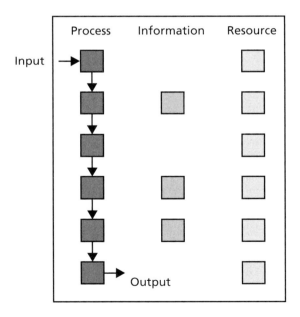

**Figure 7.6 – Simple process mapping**

When the mapping has been completed for all the processes that support the critical activities for key products or services, it is possible to identify all the resources that are used to support these activities (see Figure 7.7).

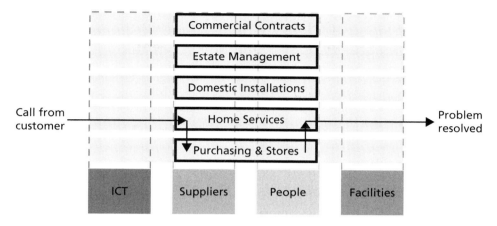

**Figure 7.7 – Mapping resources to critical activities**

The inputs and outputs are recorded together with the timescales and the resources used to complete the task. The resources are recorded against the individual process elements. As previously stated, it is important to recognize that some activities are seasonal and that the use of resources may vary throughout the year, e.g. Christmas mail requires temporary staff and additional facilities.

Appendix H provides a template for recording resources against activities.

## Risk Assessment (RA)

It is now possible to undertake risk assessments against the resources identified from the process mapping. Traditional risk assessment techniques are used, and using the process mapping data it is easy to identify which processes and hence which activities will be affected by a single point of failure, e.g. a key member of staff, building or supplier.

A manufacturer in the North East of England made a range of office furniture. One factory line produced a high volume, low profit margin, general office range while another made the executive range in low volumes but with high margins. It was the company's ability to supply both ranges that resulted in contracts with major organizations. When analysing the risks to the executive range it was realized that the production line had a single point of failure. It had only one, very elderly employee who was capable of applying the wood veneers to this key range of furniture and without him the line would stop. Failure to deliver the executive furniture to organizations could result in the loss of the general office furniture contract with those companies.

Lesson: identify single points of failure and ensure you have an appropriate risk treatment in place.

Internal and external threats, liabilities and exposures are identified, together with the likelihood of the threat occurring. The results must be recorded. A risk register may already exist as part of the organization's risk management system and consideration should be given to establishing one integrated risk register.

The results of the business impact analysis and risk analysis are then used to create a risk matrix for the critical activities as shown in Figure 7.8.

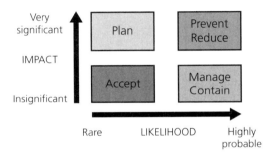

**Figure 7.8 – Example of a risk matrix**

The high-level working group or senior manager is again consulted to seek agreement on the assignment of the risks to the critical activities. It is also important to understand what level of risk the organization is prepared to accept: the risk appetite. This will determine the level of resilience required and the amount of delay that is acceptable before continuity of operations is achieved.

## Risk treatments

From the risk assessment matrix in Figure 7.8 it can be seen that there are a number of options that can be applied to the critical activities: accept, manage or contain, reduce or prevent and plan. An appropriate risk treatment may be to implement one or a combination of these.

### Accept

Where the impact is insignificant and the likelihood of failure is rare the high-level working group may decide to accept the risk and do nothing. This is a perfectly acceptable course of action and is driven by the risk appetite of the organization. The risk appetite will vary according to the size and style of the organization, the stakeholders and their interests, the sector in which it operates, the behaviour of competitors and the senior management's own approach to risk.

## Mitigate

Where the risk level is high but the impact on the critical activity is low the best option is to mitigate the risk, which is to say manage or contain the risk. If the risk of power failure is high then the provision of a standby generator and uninterrupted power supply will minimize the impact on critical activities. If the use of a single supplier would stop the activity then a second supplier would provide appropriate resilience to minimize the risk.

> The River Severn at Bewdley in Worcestershire is very prone to flooding. The properties adjacent to the river have suffered much damage over the years and as a result find it virtually impossible to obtain flood insurance.
>
> The owner of the local fish and chip shop decided to modify his equipment to reduce risks and thus minimize his losses. He obtained fridges that had their electrical equipment mounted on the top of the cabinets and fitted his fryer with hydraulic jacks to raise it above the flood level. While not preventing the flood he protected his equipment and ensured a speedy return to normal once the waters receded.

## Stop, cease or suspend

Where the likelihood of failure is very high and the impact would be considerable on the organization, urgent action will be needed. If it is not possible to reduce the risk then a decision may be taken to cease the activity. This may not be possible if it is a statutory requirement, e.g. to fight fires. Alternatives are to change or re-engineer the processes that support the activities or to transfer to an alternative location where the risk may be lower, e.g. away from a flood plain.

## Plan for continuity

Where the risk of failure is low but the impact would be high it is essential that consideration be given to continuity and incident management plans that could deal with such a situation if it should arise. An example would be the classic case of a group of key staff winning the national lottery and all failing to report for work.

Appendix I provides a template for recording risks and mitigation strategies.

Insurance is often seen as a way of offsetting the consequences of some threats if they should occur. Although insurance can compensate for loss of facilities and earnings it will not protect brand and reputation. As customer loyalty has weakened in recent years, organizations will have to consider how they will continue to service clients and customers while facilities are being rebuilt.

Business continuity planning is an element of the BCM process that is designed to ensure the organization can continue to deliver its products and services to clients and customers. The depth of planning applied depends upon the level of risk and the impact on the organization of any disruption, as well as the risk appetite of the organization's executive.

The outcome of the risk assessments should be a set of risk treatments that are designed to reduce the likelihood of disruption, shorten the period of disruption if it should happen and limit the impact of any disruption on the organization's key products and services.

Both business impact analysis and risk analysis must be reviewed at planned intervals and when significant changes occur to the organization or the environment in which it operates.

# 8. Determining business continuity strategies

Having identified the critical activities, processes and resources that support the key products or services of the organization, completed the impact and risk assessments and agreed the recovery time objectives, together with the minimum level of service required, it is time to consider how continuity of operation will be achieved.

There are four elements to this stage of the process as set out in BS 25999-2:

1. develop and document an incident response structure;
2. determine how the organization will recover each critical activity within the RTO and the resources required to do so;
3. determine how relationships with key stakeholders will be managed at the time of disruption;
4. take account of those activities not defined as critical.

## Incident response structure

The term 'incident' has been used in both parts of BS 25999 but could be replaced with 'crisis' or 'emergency'. Every organization, regardless of size, must have a procedure in place to deal with a disruptive event.

An IRS (incident response structure) supports all levels of activities that take place during a disruptive event. If no structure exists there is a danger that response, continuity and eventual recovery plans will be operated independently of each other. This may cause delays, conflicts, incorrect allocation of resources and failure to achieve required levels of continuity.

It is critical that the organization moves at the speed of the incident in order to maintain control of the situation. In a larger organization it is strongly recommended that separation exists between the team that manages the emergency situation, e.g. fire and evacuation, and the team responsible for ensuring continuity of operations. The mistake has been made in the public sector of having the same individuals trying to manage a public emergency situation, e.g. flooding, and also trying to manage the authority's own continuity. This has proved to be impractical and exhausting for the management team involved.

Procedures must be appropriate to the size and nature of the organization and set out the basis for determining when a disruption has occurred and how plans will be invoked. The timeline for response is shown in Figure 8.1. The diagram indicates a sequential implementation of incident, continuity and recovery plans. However, in some cases the plans may be implemented in rapid succession or simultaneously.

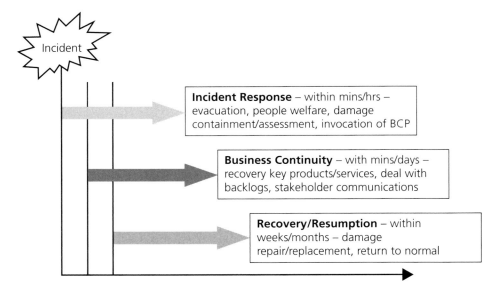

**Figure 8.1 – Incident response timeline**

There are four elements within a good IRS:

1. situation assessment;
2. IRS activation;
3. communication capability;
4. decision-making processes.

## Assessment

The incident procedure must identify the authority that determines the scale and severity of the disruption. There must be a process in place for undertaking an initial assessment of the situation together with an ongoing process of monitoring and reporting to those who are managing the incident.

## Activation

The IRS must specify the process to be used to activate the plans, who should be consulted and who should be informed. Authority for activation should be invested at the appropriate level. If the disruption is at business unit level then the local manager should have the authority to invoke the plan. Investing the authority for invocation at a high level might not be appropriate and could delay the response, causing the situation to get out of control and lead to serious consequences for the organization.

> For six days in January 1998 freezing rain coated large parts of Canada, resulting in 7–11 cm of ice being deposited on telephone and power cables. The weight of the ice brought down poles and transmission towers causing massive power and telephone outages that left 4 million people without electricity supply, some for as long as a month. The authority to invoke the power company's emergency plan was vested in the senior executives who were still away in their holiday homes. They could not be contacted as the landline communications to their remote locations were lost. This delayed the company's response to the emergency.
>
> Lesson: ensure there is always someone on duty who has the authority to invoke the plan.

## Communication

If the plans are invoked it is essential that all interested parties are informed and kept up to date. Who is to be informed and who will manage communication must be established as part of the IRS. This would include the media if appropriate: a media spokesperson should be nominated in the IRS. Clear and concise communication is required at the time of disruption. This is covered fully later in this chapter.

## Decision making

It is important that at the time of a major disruption the organization has in place a structure that will allow the management to make informed decisions and to take control of the situation. Organizations whose management style is normally based on debate and consensus will have to switch to a command and control structure (see Figure 8.2). The emergency services and military have no problem with this approach as it is their normal management system. Other organizations will have problems with this approach if it has not been rehearsed before an incident occurs.

The model shown in Figure 8.2 is suitable for large and medium-sized organizations. An SME (small and medium-sized enterprise) will have limited management resources to allocate to tactical and strategic responsibilities. In these circumstances it is essential that those who are managing the incident take time to address levels 1 and 2, notwithstanding the pressing issues at an operational level.

At the time of a major disruption it is possible that conflicting priorities will arise as resources will be limited and all managers believe their activities are critical. The decisions about priorities should have been made at the planning stage and not at the time of the disruption. However, every situation is different and there must be a mechanism in place to adjust priorities accordingly. The strategic BCM team must be empowered to determine priorities and therefore should be assembled from people who understand and represent the organization.

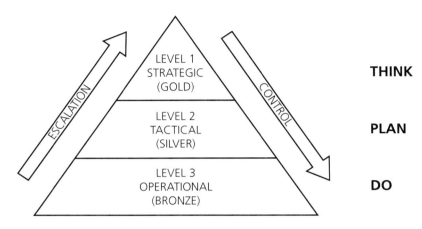

Figure 8.2 – Model of a command and control structure

## Continuity options

The next stage is for the organization to determine how it will recover each critical activity within the RTO and the resources required to do so. In choosing the appropriate option or strategy, consideration must be given to the maximum tolerable period of disruption for each activity, the costs of implementing the strategy and the consequences of inaction.

In setting the strategies consideration must be given to how they involve key resources, e.g. people, premises, technology, information and supplies. Information was considered separately from technology in undertaking the process mapping outlined in Chapter 7 as with access to critical information, regardless of the availability of the technology, it might be possible to run a key service manually.

A company in the south-east of the UK was an important supplier of an essential product to a large meat processor in East Anglia. Its factory was located in a small town and the power to the factory was from the only electricity substation in the area. Not unusually the power was interrupted one morning so production stopped. Normally the power was restored in approximately one hour but this morning it stayed off. On contacting the supply company the managing director was informed that the substation had burnt out and it would be at least two days before restoration.

This caused the company a major problem. It had no power for its computers, phone system, fax, office or warehouse. It had no paper records as everything was computer-based and there was no back up. As a consequence the company could not access customer, staff or supplier records. Although it had products in the warehouse the staff did not know what was to be despatched where and could not access the warehouse anyway without lighting. Having sent the staff home the company could not contact them to advise what it required them to do. Meanwhile the customer had tons of meat awaiting processing at its plant.

Lesson: always ensure you have access to key information that is not dependent upon a functioning computer system.

The company featured above has now installed a small generator to provide resilience.

It is recommended that four scenarios are considered when developing strategies. The cause that lies behind the scenario should not be considered. Instead it is the impact if they should occur that should be taken into account. The four scenarios are:

1. denial of access to plant or premises;
2. shortage of staff;
3. failure of technology;
4. failure of a key supplier or partner.

There are three levels at which strategies can be set:

1. Full availability – cannot fail.
2. Recovery within RTO at an agreed minimum level.
3. Do nothing.

Full availability is provided where any disruption to the activity cannot be tolerated. Examples are 999 emergency call answering, e-banking activities or the A&E department in a hospital. Duplication of the activities and the resources that support them is the most appropriate way to achieve full availability. This may involve the provision of a second online computer facility at a separate site running in parallel with the primary site, served by a duplicated telecommunications network.

Where resumption of the activity can be phased over a period of time, it is possible to agree levels of resumption at fixed points in time. Consideration of the impact on the organization of the disruption over time will set the parameters for this approach, e.g. 25 per cent (minimum level agreed) to be available in two hours, 50 per cent in two days, full service in one week.

Examples of solutions that meet this approach are: standby offices equipped with PCs and telephones where staff delivering critical activities can be accommodated at short notice;

alternative suppliers or buffer stocks; the use of interim managers to fill critical posts; and reciprocal arrangements with a similar organization.

If the strategy to be used is based on full availability, or alternatively recovery within RTO at an agreed minimum level, then the type and amount of resources needed to achieve this have to be identified. Appendix J provides a basis for recording resource requirements while Appendix K sets out possible strategies that relate to the organization's key resources.

Doing nothing is an acceptable option. However, there are implications that, if not managed, will subsequently have a serious impact on the organization. This may be financial or, more likely, will affect reputation. In preparing the case for this option it is important to identify the range of impacts that will arise over time and establish appropriate actions to counteract them, e.g. communications to stakeholders as to why the decision to do nothing has been taken. An example of such a strategy would be a local authority suspending the processing of planning applications in the event of an emergency in the community.

## Backlog trap

If the decision is to suspend or reduce the level of activity for a particular set of services or products then arrangements must be made to 'catch up' by carrying out the outstanding work that has built up during the disruption. This may involve overtime working, outsourcing work or even deciding not to resume work at all. Organizations that managed to weather a disruption have subsequently failed by not being able to overcome the backlog of work.

A small, regional broadband communications supplier was attracting many new customers as a result of their pricing policies. As more customers were signed up their system response slowed down. This resulted in a large number of customer complaints to the already stretched customer service staff. An upgrade to the system was initiated but this resulted in more complaints as problems arose with the installation.

New call centre staff were recruited but went live before being fully trained. The number of outstanding complaints escalated even further. At this point the media became involved. The company could no longer keep on top of complaints and the backlog built up to such an extent that customers began leaving. Eventually the company was forced to sell out to a national provider.

There will be cost implications for each strategy chosen. Wherever possible these must be set against the cost of disruption. It must be appreciated that in some cases financial costs cannot be applied to the impact of the disruption on the activity. It may be that the greatest impact would be damage to reputation or embarrassment for elected representatives.

## Communication strategies

If the organization suffers a major disruption it is essential to provide appropriate communication to stakeholders. This will be internal and external. All stakeholders have expectations they place on the organization and will be concerned about how they will be affected by the disruption being suffered by the organization.

> When a major computer manufacturer suffered a software load problem on its PC production line it shut the line for three days. It operated a policy of 'build to order' and customers were given a date and time for delivery. The company chose not to inform customers of the problem unless the customer directly contacted them. The main IT weekly newspaper picked up the story and the subsequent publicity was damaging to the manufacturer.
>
> Lesson: if you intend to do nothing then make certain you have informed those who are expecting service or product delivery.

The evidence from research undertaken by Knight and Pretty of Templeton College, Oxford, in the mid-1990s (Knight and Pretty, 2000) shows that those organizations that ignore the importance of communicating with their stakeholders are the most likely to suffer the greatest impact from any major incident.

The stakeholders and their interests were identified at the start of the BCM process. Using the output from this analysis the organization must establish appropriate strategies to manage the relationships with key stakeholders.

Particular emphasis should be placed on communication with staff, as they will be concerned about their welfare and employment. At the time of disruption clear communication is required to advise staff of what actions to take. This can be done through hard copy, internet, local media or recorded messages on a freephone number.

Arrangements must be made to keep senior management informed about the progress towards resumption. It is essential to identify who within the organization will be responsible for planning and delivering communication.

One key element of a communication strategy is how the organization will manage the media at the time of a major disruption. Regardless of the size of the organization, if the event is significant enough to raise the media's interest someone must be appointed to act as the organization's spokesperson. Preparing material that can be quickly adapted when needed will save time. This should include draft response statements and general information about the organization. How this is managed must be developed as part of the communication strategy.

The decision on what levels of resilience and continuity are to be applied within the organization falls to the executive and/or the high-level working group. They will make their decision based on the level of risk and their appetite for risk. The executive and/or the high-level working group must sign off strategies to support the key products or services, as well as critical activities and their supporting resources, acknowledging the cost implications, before any planning activities can commence.

# 9. Developing and implementing a BCM response

The first action for many organizations has been to create a business continuity plan without going through the key steps outlined in Chapters 7 and 8. The danger in taking this approach is that it will not result in a true understanding of the organization and how it delivers key products or services. Consideration of various strategies and their resource requirements may have been missed. As a result the plan produced may not be fit for purpose and not offer the protection and benefits that would have been possible. By completing the processes set out in Chapters 7 and 8 the organization can now develop realistic and appropriate incident and business continuity plans.

Experience has shown that organizations can be disrupted for many reasons. Business continuity planning has traditionally been based on known threats: loss of IT, loss of a building through fire, flooding, etc. In recent times, however, the UK has experienced some unexpected disruptions, including a widespread outbreak of foot and mouth disease, extensive disruptions to the rail network, a national shortage of oil-based fuels and the loss of water supplies for weeks. In most cases existing plans did not cover these disruptions and the impact they had on organizations.

When developing plans it is important that all elements of the organization are involved (see Figure 9.1). If this does not happen assumptions will be made about the ability of other parts of the organization to respond and meet the needs of the plan. If the plan calls for members of staff to work from home then the IT department must confirm that technical arrangements have or can be made to enable this to happen. The human resources department may need to adjust their policies to accommodate remote working and health and safety policies may have to be modified.

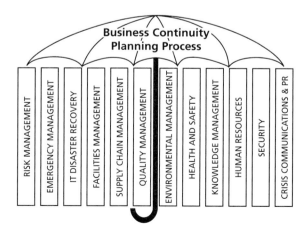

**Figure 9.1 – Involving everyone in the planning process (source: Sharp, 1999)**

Plans should provide answers to basic questions:

- What is to be done?
- When?
- Where are the alternative resources located?
- Who is involved?
- How is continuity to be achieved?

In any organization there may be a suite of interconnected plans covering emergency, business continuity, incident management and recovery management. The plans produced should be appropriate for the organization. A small organization, operating from one site, may only need a single document that covers incident management and continuity management, while larger organizations will need integrated corporate, divisional and business unit plans based on a common structure. Such plans must be synchronized to eliminate conflicts and ensure that agreed restoration priorities are achieved. In a large organization a central BCM team or BCM co-ordinator undertakes this role.

BS 25999 identifies two areas of planning that must be in place as part of a BCMS, incident management and continuity management.

## Incident response structure

BS 25999-2 states that 'the organization shall identify incident response personnel, who shall have the necessary seniority, authority and competence to take control of the situation and communicate with stakeholders' (BS 25999-2:2007).

As stated in Chapter 8, the strategic team must be empowered to determine priorities and therefore should be assembled from people in positions who understand and represent the organization. They should have access to the information required to confirm the nature and extent of the disruption and to the plans for activation, operation, co-ordination and communication of the response to the incident. They also need access to appropriate resources to support the management of the incident.

Full details of the incident response structure are set out in Chapter 8.

## Plans

The organization will need to create plans that detail how it will manage the incident (incident response plans) and how it will achieve continuity of operations (business continuity plans) that are based on the previously agreed timescales and levels of production or service.

Plans will be subject to change and therefore version control and configuration management must be applied. Each copy of the plan must be numbered and controlled distribution established. Where sensitive information is contained in the plan it must be given the appropriate level of confidentiality.

Plans may take various formats. They may be written as text or flow charts or produced by specialist software. They can be internet and/or paper-based, held on a PDA or in a simple 'wallet' format. Plans should not be vast documents as they will be used in times of stress and therefore should be kept as straightforward as possible, containing the minimum amount of information to enable the team to deliver continuity. They must be accessible at all times to those named individuals who are required to use them.

> On several occasions when major incidents have occurred in London the police have been forced to evacuate and cordon off large areas of commercial districts. Individuals were found trying to cross the cordon lines to get access to their building. When challenged they informed the authorities that they needed to get their business continuity plan as it had been left in the office.
>
> Lesson: make certain there are copies of incident and continuity plans available at all times and that additional copies are kept off site.

Within a large organization a common template may be used for the creation of incident and continuity plans. There are frequent requests from organizations for standard templates to be published by regulatory and statutory bodies that just require 'box filling'. While a template is useful as a guideline, it must be recognized that no two organizations are the same and even separate locations within the same organization will have differences. The plan must therefore reflect the organization rather than the organization being made to fit a standard template.

Ownership of the plan must be identified. In larger organizations there will be plans at different levels. Business unit managers should own operational plans. All plans must be reviewed regularly and also when significant changes occur to the organization or the environment in which it operates. The responsible owner must undertake the review that is then signed off at a higher level.

The plans must also take account of any external arrangements for managing an incident. These include the actions of the emergency services, local authorities and other external agencies in the event of a major disruption and, if sharing a building, the contingency arrangements of the facilities management company or landlord.

## Plan contents

The following sections discuss the recommended elements of incident response and business continuity plans.

## Purpose and scope

These should be defined.

## Roles and responsibilities

The plan should identify the roles and responsibilities of those post holders who will be involved in delivering the plan. It will identify the team leader, key team members and their deputies to be assembled at the time of invocation. It will set out their levels of authority (including financial authority) and to whom they must report their actions. It will also set out the point at which the responsibility for incident management must pass to a higher level in the organization. There may be separate teams responsible for incident and continuity plans.

## Invoking the plan

The plan must indicate the circumstances under which it is to be invoked and who can authorize the invocation. It must also include details of how to manage a disruption and its impact upon the organization. It is essential that an organization responds quickly if a crisis or disaster is to be avoided. The invocation of a business unit plan may need a lower level of authority to deal with a local incident. It is important that any invocation is flagged to senior management so it is aware that an incident exists and can consider the wider implications for the organization. Instructions to that effect should be written into the plan.

Call-out lists (call trees) should be included in the plan along with details of where the team should proceed to in order to manage the disruption (command centre). The command centre should be equipped with the appropriate level of communications and other facilities to allow the incident to be managed effectively. 'Battle boxes' can be provided that include essential resources to assist the continuity team commence action plus documentation that supports the plan.

## Alternative locations

Details of standby locations should be included, together with maps, security arrangements to gain access, contractual terms and any other relevant information.

## System recovery plans

Small companies may include basic system recovery plans within the main document. These may consist of instructions on how to restore data or transfer telecommunication services to an alternative location. In larger organizations the recovery plans will be complex and will be separate documents owned by the unit responsible for providing the service, e.g. IT recovery plans for a major data centre. The main plan should identify the recovery plan owners and the key actions they will take.

## Contact details

The plan should include full details for internal and external contacts. These may include:

- key senior management;
- key operational staff;
- emergency services;
- local authority officers;
- regulators and other compliance bodies;
- suppliers;
- key customers;
- utility companies;
- insurers;
- media organizations.

It may be appropriate to include details of contracts, insurance policies, regulatory requirements, etc. These additional documents may be stored separately to the plan itself but should be accessible.

## Priorities

Details of the priority order for continuity and recovery of key products or services and their critical activities must be available together with their RTOs and recovery levels.

## Vital documents and resources

A list of vital documents and resources needed for continuity and recovery for each critical activity must be included along with details of where these are located. These should be based on the output from the BIA. Vital documents may include records of who is authorized to retrieve materials as well as security arrangements, e.g. passwords that will be required. Vital materials may include stationery, spare parts, specialist machinery and tools.

## Checklists and audit trails

A simple checklist or action card may be included to ensure the team completes mandatory tasks and provides a tracking process for task completion. Meeting agendas can be included so that all key elements of the plan are covered when the team meets.

With any major incident there will be a requirement for post-event inquiry and audit. It is vital therefore that a record is maintained of what actions were taken, why they were taken, when they were taken and by whom. This is the incident log, an example of which is given in Appendix L.

## People issues

Special consideration must be given to the needs of staff, contractors and visitors who may have been evacuated from the normal premises without time to collect their personal belongings, e.g. money, credit cards, keys and identity cards. There may be injuries or deaths and immediate family would have to be informed. The organization has a duty of care to its staff and these personnel issues will need to be addressed as part of the incident plan, which must identify whose responsibility it is to deal with the people issues.

Plans must also take account of the welfare of those who will be managing the disruption, comply with health and safety requirements and ensure there are sufficient team members available to work shifts in the event of the disruption extending over a long period.

## Public profile

Reputation and brand image are valuable assets for any organization, whether a multinational, SME, a public or voluntary body. Major disruptions will attract the interest of the media, which will judge how well the organization is handling the situation and will expose and exploit any weakness or mistake very quickly to the wider world. An element of the plan should be devoted to protecting the public face of the organization. Larger organizations may choose to have a separate incident communication plan to cover this area (see Chapter 8).

## Salvage

This is an area frequently omitted from BCM. If the organization has suffered fire, flooding or other damage to its buildings then it is important to ensure that, when safe to do so, arrangements are made to recover important documents and equipment. Documents and equipment that are damaged by water or other contaminants can be cleaned and restored by specialist contractors. As time is of the essence it will assist with recovery if there are pre-existing arrangements in place with appropriate contractors to carry out such restoration work.

> When Carlisle was flooded in January 2005 the police station was severely affected. Evidence relating to pending prosecutions stored in the basement was not only soaked

but also contaminated by sewage. There was a danger that this evidence would be lost forever. However, a document recovery company was called to effect a salvage. They were able to dry and clean all the material and not one single case was lost due to loss of evidence.

There are two lessons to be learnt from this case. The first is to ensure that key documentation is stored in a location that is safe and where it will not be subject to external contamination. The second is that if the worst does occur there are organizations that can recover badly damaged documents. Identifying such organizations prior to their being required will save time and perhaps ensures your organization has priority.

## Returning to normal

A process must exist for standing down the incident and continuity teams and returning to normal once the disruption is over.

Effective continuity plans are written on the basis of recovering the critical activities of the organization whatever the cause of the disruption. Plans should provide a framework for achieving restoration. As the plans are used under challenging and stressful circumstances they should be concise, simple and easy to follow. In addition plans should ensure the organization maintains compliance with applicable laws and regulations during the period of their implementation.

## Long-term recovery plans

Following a major disruption, e.g. a fire that destroys an office building, plans have to be made to replace the facility through relocation or rebuild. The continuity plans will have ensured that key products and services are maintained at agreed levels but this may only be appropriate in the short term. Long-term recovery will need to be managed as a major project and such plans will be separate from those covered by the BCMS system. As Figure 8.1 showed, recovery planning may start very soon after the incident has occurred but a separate long-term recovery team should be assembled to manage the project.

When the Aulds bakery in Scotland, which produces frozen desserts for the UK retail market, was destroyed by fire the management team knew they had eight weeks of product in freezers and customers' facilities. In the eight-week window the company was able to build a temporary factory adjacent to the fire-damaged premises and get back into production.

It had formed a team dedicated to managing the immediate recovery that obtained a temporary structure, erected it adjacent to the old factory and equipped it with all the specialist plant required. It was then able to plan the long-term recovery, eventually moving into a new plant 15 months after the fire. Customers remained loyal to the company as it kept them informed of progress throughout the recovery.

## Implementation

Having completed the plans, they must be implemented. Those who hold positions that are named in the plan must be made aware of their role and have the appropriate training to enable them to fulfil their responsibilities. The section on training in Chapter 4 and the key questions for establishing a training programme, set out in Appendix E, provide useful guidance on training. Exercising plans is one of the principal methods of ensuring that those who will be involved in managing an incident and effecting continuity are aware of the contents of the plan and their roles. Exercising is covered in Chapter 10.

Appropriate stakeholders, both internal and external, need to be aware that the organization has plans in place to deal with disruptions. They need to be conscious of what will be done, what products and services will be available and at what levels. Where appropriate, they also need to know what the organization will not be doing while it recovers.

External stakeholders, partners and suppliers, who have a role to play in assisting the organization cope with disruption, need to know their role and responsibilities in supporting the organization's requirements. As these partners and suppliers may also be affected by the same disruption it is important that they have plans to maintain their own continuity of service.

Appendix M shows an example of a possible plan structure. It is important to note that plans must be appropriate to the organization and support the management of a disruptive incident, not hinder it. A simple action card might be appropriate at the business unit level to commence the incident response, with the full plans being held at the command centre locations.

# 10. Exercising and maintaining

## Exercising

BCM requires that effective plans be established to ensure an organization can respond to any incident. But the process does not stop at the planning stage. Plans are worthless unless they are rehearsed. Many examples exist where organizations have business continuity plans in place but the plans fail because they have not been rehearsed. In the UK, research has shown that only 46 per cent of those organizations with plans test or rehearse on an annual basis while 21 per cent never rehearse their plans at all (see Figure 10.1).

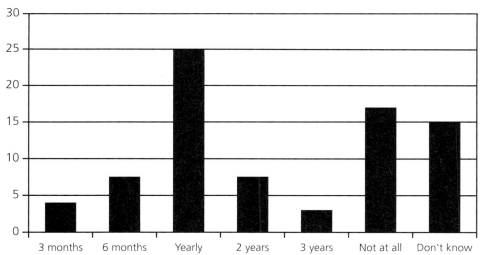

**Frequency of business continuity plan rehearsal**

**Figure 10.1 – Frequency with which UK organizations rehearse business continuity plans (source: Chartered Management Institute, 2006)**

The rehearsal of plans is essential as it is highly unlikely that any plan created will work first time. Rehearsing ensures that disconnections and omissions within the plan are fixed before it is used in reality. 89 per cent of those organizations that rehearsed found errors in their plans. It is far better to have found the errors at rehearsal than the first time the plan is invoked in response to a real incident. Having found the errors it is essential that time-specified actions are created to rectify the errors and omissions. Figure 10.2 shows the latest results of rehearsals for UK organizations.

**Errors found in business continuity plan rehearsals**

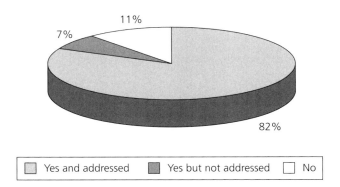

| | | |
|---|---|---|
| ☐ Yes and addressed | ■ Yes but not addressed | ☐ No |

**Figure 10.2 – Results of BCM rehearsals
(source: Chartered Management Institute, 2007)**

Exercising helps to build confidence in team members by clarifying roles and responsibilities, supplying practical training and awareness as well as providing valuable experience of responding to an incident.

There are various forms of rehearsals but it important to:

• test the systems;
• exercise the plans;
• rehearse the people.

Examples of tests for systems may be to ensure that the standby generator starts when power is interrupted, that the telephone divert arrangements work or that data can be recovered from the back-up source.

> The managing director of a small company that relied on IT systems ensured that a back up of important data was taken every day, copied onto a tape. He took the tape home every night, placing it in a door side pocket in his car.
>
> When a problem occurred with the company's server attempts were made to use the back-up tape to recover the data. Unfortunately there was no data on the tape. By placing the tape in the door pocket it had been adjacent to one of the car's loudspeakers and the magnetic field generated by the loudspeaker had wiped the data from the tape.
>
> Lessons: tapes should be stored in a safe off-site environment, there should be more than one copy and regular data restore tests should be undertaken.

Testing should ensure that technical systems work correctly and that operating instructions are clear and valid for the equipment. The tests should be as close to live working as possible, e.g. full load being taken by the generator. Another form of test that should be carried out on a regular basis is a 'call cascade'. This is used to verify lines of communication that will be used when invoking the plans.

Plans should be exercised to ensure they are comprehensive and realistic. The first exercise should be one to 'prove the plan works' and should be sold as a learning exercise. Prior to this first exercise it is advisable for the plan to be read by someone who has not been involved in producing the document. This is to ensure the plan is clear and makes sense to others, to check that it takes account of all the people involved and to spot any gaps in the document.

Exercising is not about achieving a pass or a fail but ensuring the plan works as intended. It is also a training opportunity for those who are named in the documents. There are certain key rules to be observed when planning exercises.

Exercises must have defined aims and objectives that may include:

• affirmation that everyone understands their role and that there is an overall appreciation of the plan;
• checking that the invocation procedures and call-out communications work;
• ensuring that the accommodation, equipment, systems and services provided are appropriate and operational;
• verifying that key products or services can be recovered within the RTO and to the levels required.

Exercises should not 'risk' the organization by causing disruptions. They must be practical and cost-effective, appropriate to the organization and designed to build confidence in the plan.

A very large public sector organization was testing the UPS (uninterruptible power supplies) that served their main computer systems. A failure occurred with the UPS that caused the mains power to the computers to trip out resulting in a complete loss of systems. In the rush to restore power, the trip switch was restored but this caused a massive spike in voltage to the computers. This burned out several key components in the computers. Alternative systems were established but full restoration took several weeks. It was acknowledged that the test had not been properly planned and no risk assessment had been undertaken.

Lesson: planning your exercise and carrying out impact and risk assessments is very important.

A regular programme of exercises should be established and documented. These should take place at a period determined by the top management or when there have been significant changes to the organization or the environment in which it operates. Observers should be appointed to note the way the incident and continuity teams handle the situation. Every effort must be made to gain full participation from those involved in the exercise. If the organization has an internal audit function there is value in inviting someone from this department to attend and provide feedback on performance against the plan.

There are various forms of exercise ranging from desktop review, where the participants review and challenge the contents of the plan, through 'walk-throughs', where the interaction between players is assessed, to full plan test where the site or building is shut down and a move undertaken to an alternative location. Full plan testing is the only way to assure all concerned parties that the incident and continuity management arrangements will work when required.

To exercise a plan the BCM management should decide upon an appropriate scenario that has relevance to the organization. Initially it may be appropriate to exercise elements of the plan separately, resolving any gaps found, before running a complete plan exercise. It is important that the scenario is changed each time the exercise is performed in order to challenge the plan and ensure all its components are examined.

As disruptions occur without warning there is benefit in running a snap exercise where only the minimum number of people are made aware that the exercise is to take place. The exercise can be run in real time or compressed time so that a plan can be exercised in one session. It is important to include time-out periods so that people and teams can clarify their understanding of the exercise. Because the exercise will require intense concentration from the players, careful consideration should be given to the length of time taken by the exercise.

Rehearsing the team players is vital. People demonstrate different characteristics when put under pressure. A real invocation will be a stressful situation and it is important to understand the strengths and weaknesses of the individuals concerned. As previously stated, in the UK the normal management culture surrounding decision making is based on consensus with the maximum information being available to all parties. At times of plan invocation the management style may have to move to command and control, working with less than perfect information.

Different leadership styles are needed and it could be that the initial teams chosen lack certain skills. Some of these can be acquired through training but often it will be necessary to change roles or even exclude people from the team. It is not always the most senior person who is best at managing a disruptive incident.

A log of all actions and outcomes must be made during the exercise and this must be reviewed as soon as possible after the event. It is a good idea for this review to be carried out with the participants so they can express their own views on what went well or otherwise. To assist with this participants should be asked to maintain their own diary of events throughout the exercise. The views of the independent observers should also be included.

A post-exercise report should be completed that includes recommendations on actions to adjust the plans. A senior manager of the unit in which the exercise was conducted should sign off the report and the actions to be taken. The process of exercising is set out in Figure 10.3.

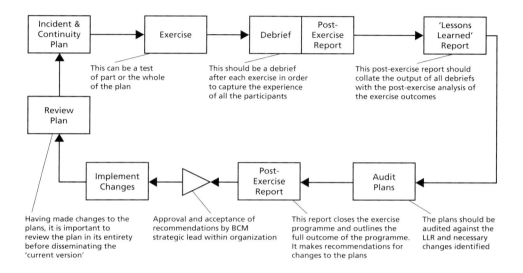

**Figure 10.3 – The exercising cycle (source: HM Government, 2005)**

Documentation from the exercise programme provides clear evidence to auditors that BCM is being taken seriously within the organization and as such would form a vital part of any documentation being submitted when seeking compliance with or certification against BS 25999-2.

## Maintaining

Nothing stands still; organizations are in a continual state of flux. Staff change roles and responsibilities; some will leave and new people will join. Mergers, acquisitions, organic growth and downsizing mean that structures and reporting lines will evolve. Suppliers and customers change, regulatory and legal environments may be adjusted; political conditions in supply countries may become unstable. An outsourcing contract may change the responsibility for critical functions, e.g. IT being outsourced to a third party. New products and services may be introduced, new sites opened or others closed. At the basic level, contact details will always be changing.

Processes must be established in the organization whereby any change that will affect business continuity is flagged up to the BCM co-ordinator or appropriate BCM lead. Adjustments to plans should be made if the changes are minor. If major changes have occurred it may be necessary to revisit the BIA to reassess critical activities and supporting processes and resources. New continuity strategies may be required and the incident and continuity plans changed. Any changes made to the BCM arrangements must be subject to the appropriate levels of sign-off.

Regardless of whether there have been changes or not, the BCM arrangements should be subject to an annual review to ensure they are still current. Senior management should review the list of key products or services and an assessment should be made about the criticality of supporting activities and their priority for recovery. Checks should be made to ensure that the supporting processes and resources are still correct. Plans should be reviewed to ensure they are still appropriate and workable. An appropriate management level should sign off the reviews regardless of whether changes have or have not been made.

Staff will need to be made aware of any changes that affect the way continuity will be achieved in the organization. As mentioned before, it is vital that version control is applied to BCM documentation and that a process exists whereby updates are issued and old versions withdrawn.

## Post-incident review

If the organization has suffered a disruptive incident that has resulted in the incident and/or continuity plans being invoked, arrangements should be in place to carry out a post-incident review to:

- establish the nature and cause of the incident;
- assess the adequacy of the management's response;
- assess the effectiveness of the plans to meet the RTOs;
- assess the capabilities of those involved in implementing the plans;
- identify any improvement that can be made to the process.

This completes the Do component of the BCMS.

# 11. Monitoring, reviewing, maintaining and improving the BCMS

This final chapter relates to the Check and Act elements of the business continuity management system. The Check element covers monitoring and reviewing while maintaining and improving the BCMS forms the Act element.

## Monitoring and reviewing the BCMS

While the final section of Chapter 10 covered the maintenance of incident management and continuity management activities, this section sets out the responsibility of the organization to review the BCMS at planned intervals or when significant changes occur to the organization or the environment in which it operates. This is required to ensure the BCMS continues to be suitable, adequate and effective. The review can be carried out through self-assessment or audits and can be undertaken either using internal resources or independent external auditors. A self-assessment checklist is included in Appendix N.

The review must look for opportunities to improve or, if appropriate, change the structure of the BCMS. Areas to be covered include those set out in Chapters 2–6, with specific attention being given to the BCM policy and objectives for the organization. The output of the reviews must be documented and records maintained.

Various sources of information can be used to inform the review. These include:

- output from BCMS audits and internal reviews;
- output from reviews of supplier and partner BCM arrangements;
- feedback from interested parties (i.e. stakeholders) and recommendations for improvements;
- developments in BCM techniques, products, procedures and good practice;
- the status of preventative and corrective actions, including follow-up actions previously identified;
- the level of residual risk and changes in the organization's risk appetite;
- emerging vulnerabilities/threats and those not previously addressed adequately;
- output from exercises, including the lessons learned reports;
- observation/recommendations from incidents or near misses experienced by the organization and others;
- results of the education and awareness programmes;
- KPIs relating to the BCMS.

As a result of the review a report must be compiled that sets out the decisions made and actions to be taken relating to the BCMS, together with timescales for implementation. The report must cover:

- improvements to achieve greater effectiveness of the system;
- necessary procedural modifications that affect business continuity, resulting from changes to the organization's business and resilience requirements, changes to business processes, changes to the levels of risk and risk appetite and changes to the external environment including regulations and legal requirements;
- the resources needed to achieve the improvements and modifications, together with funding and budgetary requirements.

## Maintaining and improving the BCMS

The final element of the PDCA cycle is Act, which involves maintaining and improving the BCMS. One of the key elements of a good management system is that it has the capacity for continual improvement. This is a key element of Deming's approach to quality management and it is also a requirement of BS 25999-2. Continual improvement is based on the Japanese philosophy of *Kaizen*, which means 'change for the better' or 'improvement'.

The concept of *Kaizen* is easy to understand. However, it is often difficult to achieve on an on going basis in an organization due to complacency, distractions, loss of focus, lack of commitment, reassigned priorities and lack of resources. To successfully implement BCM an organization must encourage a climate that fosters continual improvement.

Tatung of Taiwan ran a television manufacturing facility in the UK. If any employee on the production line found a problem with quality, component shortage or production methods they were authorized to stop the line. Providing the problem was genuine, the employee was not blamed for loss of production but praised for possibly preventing faulty products from being produced.

Those working within or who are closely associated with an organization are an excellent source of suggestions for improvements. They can see areas where corrections can be made to systems and preventative measures can be built in to increase overall resilience. More often than not, however, the climate within the organization is such that they are reluctant to bring their suggestions to management.

Organizations need to encourage a process whereby individuals feel able to highlight omissions, duplications and failings without being rebutted or blamed in any way. It is those who work at the 'coal face' who frequently know the solutions but the culture of the organization may prevent their ideas from surfacing. By using a suggestions scheme or discussing how BCM and the organization's resilience can be strengthened at team meetings and on a one-to-one basis, managers will be able to create a climate where continual improvement is the norm.

There are two actions associated with the final element of the BCMS: correction and prevention.

## Corrective actions

This is where the organization eliminates the cause of nonconformities associated with the BCMS in order to prevent their recurrence. BS 25999-2 sets out the documented procedures for corrective actions. These must define the requirements for:

- identifying any nonconformities;
- determining the causes of nonconformities;
- evaluating the need for actions to ensure that nonconformities do not recur;
- determining and implementing the corrective action needed;
- recording the results of action taken;
- reviewing the corrective action taken.

## Preventative actions

Having identified and dealt with nonconformities the organization must take steps to guard against recurrence of these nonconformities. Any preventative actions must be appropriate to the impact of the potential problems and must not inhibit the BCMS process. BS 25999-2 sets out the documented procedures for preventative actions. These must define the requirements for:

- identifying potential nonconformities and their causes;
- determining and implementing preventative actions needed;
- recording the results of action taken;
- reviewing any preventative action taken;
- identifying changed risks and ensuring that attention is focused on significantly changed risks;
- ensuring that all those who need to know are informed of the nonconformity and preventative action is put in place;
- determining the priority of preventative actions based on the results of the risk assessments and the BIA.

## Continual improvement

Like any management system BCMS must be subject to continual improvement. The organization must make arrangements to ensure that it continually improves the effectiveness of the BCMS through the review of the business continuity policy and objectives, audit results, analysis of monitored events, corrective and preventative actions and management review.

# 12. Conclusion

Despite the increased use of BCM in organizations, there are still managers who continue to dismiss the need for continuity management even in the face of such major disasters as the 2007 floods in the UK. Many have a strong belief that insurance will provide cover for any loss that they may suffer. This is not the case as losses are not restricted to material damage but also include loss of reputation, revenues and customers. Research has shown that for every £30 of total loss incurred only £1 is recovered through insurance and the gap between the real cost of disasters and insurance payments is considerable.

Organizations can be disrupted in many ways. Incidents include fire, flood, water shortages, storm damage, internal and external vandalism or fraud, the failure of systems and loss of data, computer hacking, machinery breakdown, failures in physical and system security and staff losses. These are only some examples. Added to this is the climate in which today's organization has to operate. The intolerance of customers and clients, their lack of loyalty and the demands of the banks for financial viability add considerable pressure at a time of disruption. If the organization is unable to manage a disruption correctly and in good time then the situation will rapidly turn into a crisis then a disaster, and the organization may fail. SMEs are at greatest risk yet they are the first to ignore the benefits of BCM. As they form the foundation on which most economies operate, it is essential that they are encouraged to adopt BCM.

As recent disasters around the world have demonstrated, it is not possible to predict all possible events that can seriously disrupt an organization's ability to maintain continuity of operations. Because the unexpected will always occur, there is a clear need to protect organizations by forward planning. Business continuity management is seen as a vital tool to achieve this. The British Standard for BCM, BS 25999, has been created to enable organizations to follow good practice as set out in the Code of practice, BS 25999-1, and to demonstrate their compliance through certification against the Specification, BS 25999-2. This book sets out to help enable any organization, regardless of sector or size, to meet the requirements of BS 25999-2. It does not claim to be a definitive guide but rather a route map that leads to the effective implementation of a business continuity management system.

# Appendix A.
# BCM drivers by sector and company size

Table A.1 – BCM drivers by company sector
(Source data: Chartered Management Institute, 2007)

| Sector | Principal drivers | Comments |
|---|---|---|
| Business services | Insurers, customers and corporate governance | Insurers are keen to reduce business interruption risks. |
| Central government | Corporate governance | While not covered by legislation it is recognized that the continuity of government departments and agencies is critical. |
| Construction | Insurers, customers and corporate governance | Major contracts are driven by project management and penalty clauses. Health and safety issues are important– insurers look for good management. |
| Education | Corporate governance | Funding bodies and auditors look for evidence of BCM. |
| Finance and insurance | Regulators, auditors and corporate governance | Industry is highly regulated and subject to a variety of audits. |
| Health and social care | Central government, legislation and corporate governance | Health services are a principal focus for government. |
| IT and telecommunications | Insurers, customers and corporate governance | IT and telecommunications provide the underpinning infrastructure for most organizations. Telecommunications are a key element of the critical national infrastructure. |
| Local government and emergency services | Central government, legislation, auditors and corporate governance | These organizations are now subject to legislation under the Civil Contingencies Act 2004. |
| Manufacturing and production | Insurers, customers and corporate governance | Major customers have become aware of their supply chain vulnerabilities while insurers are keen to reduce business interruption risks. |

| Retail/wholesale | Insurers and customers | Retail outlets drive the wholesalers but the outlets themselves have many customers who individually have no voice. |
|---|---|---|
| Transport and logistics | Customers, regulators, insurers and corporate governance | Major players in supply chain logistics. |
| Utilities – electricity, gas, water | Regulators, insurers, auditors, customers and corporate governance | Critical infrastructure operated and maintained by regulated companies who have major customers. Subject to a variety of audits. |
| Business services | Insurers and customers | Insurers are keen to reduce business interruption risks. |

## Table A.2 – BCM drivers by company size
### (Source data: Chartered Management Institute, 2005)

| Company size | Principal drivers | Comments |
|---|---|---|
| Up to £1m | No major drivers | Smaller companies are way down the supply chain. |
| £1m–£10m | Insurers and customers | The pressures at this level have started to appear from these two groups. |
| £10m–£100m | Insurers and auditors | Insurers are keen to reduce business interruption risks with this size of company where they have greater exposure. |
| £100m–£500m | Central government, auditors, legislation, insurers, customers and corporate governance | This group includes many local authorities and PLCs. |
| Over £500m | Central government, auditors, legislation, regulators, insurers, customers and corporate governance | Listed and highly regulated companies. Critical organizations in UK economy. |

# Appendix B.
# Sample scoping document

---

**ACME ORGANIZATION LTD**

**BUSINESS CONTINUITY MANAGEMENT SCOPE**

This document sets out the scope of the BCMS (business continuity management system) that is currently operated by Acme Organization Ltd.

The BCMS covers the key services of the Home Service and Commercial Contracts divisions of the organization.

The key services are:

- emergency call-out;
- fault reporting and repair.

These services are delivered from the four regional depots based in London, Birmingham, Manchester and Glasgow.

The BCMS extends to cover all resources and dependencies utilized by these key services.

The Acme Organization Ltd BCMS has been certified by XXX Group against the British Standard Specification for business continuity management, BS 25999-2.

This scoping document was issued on 10 October 2007 and will be reviewed not later than 1 October 2009

Signed on behalf of Acme Organization Ltd

.................................................................. Dated: 1 October 2007

A B Jones, Managing Director
Acme Organization Ltd
Jubilee Business Park
West Acton
London

---

**Figure B.1 – Sample scoping document**

---

# Appendix C.
# Sample business continuity policy

---

**ACME ORGANIZATION LTD**

**BUSINESS CONTINUITY POLICY**

## Introduction

The Acme Organization's business continuity policy provides the framework within which our company can comply with the business continuity requirements of our customers by introducing a business continuity management system that aligns with BS 25999-2. Business continuity management is being established to ensure our company can continue to deliver a minimum level of service to our key customers in the event of any disruption. Plans must be made, published and tested for key services as agreed by the Business Continuity Committee.

## Application

The policy applies to those divisions and areas of our company set out in the scoping document. All employees within these divisions and areas must be aware of this policy. This policy applies in particular to heads of divisions and business unit managers.

## Purpose

The Acme Organization's business continuity policy provides a structure through which:

- a comprehensive BCMS (business continuity management system) is established and maintained;
- key services, together with their supporting critical activities, processes and resources, will be identified;
- business impact analysis and risk assessment will be applied to our key services and their supporting critical activities, processes and resources;

Acme Organization business continuity policy, Version 1      Sept 2007

---

**Figure C.2 – Sample business continuity policy: Page 1**

---

- risk mitigation strategies will be applied to reduce the impact of disruption on key services;
- plans will be developed to ensure continuity of key services at a minimum acceptable standard following disruption;
- invocation of business continuity plans can be managed;
- plans are subject to ongoing exercising and revision;
- the executive board can be assured that the BCMS remains up to date and relevant.

## Policy statement

- Each key service within our company is to be owned by a designated division. The head of division will ensure that plans capable of maintaining a minimum acceptable standard of service delivery are in place for each key service.
- Supporting departments will provide professional support to improve resilience of critical activities and resources that support key services.
- Each division will carry out an annual review of its business continuity process. The Business Continuity Committee will monitor the review process, benchmark the results and provide support where necessary.
- Each division must exercise its business continuity plans at least once a year and make modifications where necessary, to take account of the exercise results.
- Contracts with suppliers of critical goods and services to our company must include a requirement for the supplier's business continuity processes to be approved and to be exercised to the satisfaction of our company.
- All staff must be made aware of the plans that affect their division or business unit and their role following invocation of business continuity plans.

## Benefits

The policy provides a clear commitment to establishing a business continuity management system within Acme Organization that will enable our company to:

- continue to provide key services to our customers in times of disruption;
- make best use of personnel and other resources at times when both may be scarce;
- reduce the period of disruption to our organization and the customers we serve;
- resume normal working more efficiently and effectively after a period of disruption;

Acme Organization business continuity policy, Version 1                    Sept 2007

**Figure C.2 – Sample business continuity policy: Page 2**

- comply with standards of corporate governance;
- improve the resilience of our organization's infrastructure to reduce the likelihood of disruption;
- reduce the operational and financial impact of any disruption.

## Responsibilities

- The Head of Finance is responsible to the executive board for business continuity issues.
- This policy is owned by the Business Continuity Committee.
- The Head of Business Continuity within the Finance Division is the professional lead for business continuity within our company and will:
  - review and develop the policy in line with industry best practice and the needs of our company;
  - monitor standards and compliance with the policy;
  - provide support and guidance to divisional managers.

## Policy review date

This policy will be subject to review by 31 October 2009.

For further enquiries please contact Head of BCM on extension 5143.

Signed on behalf of Acme Organization Ltd, Jubilee Business Park, West Acton, London

.................................................................. Dated: 1 October 2007

A B Jones, Managing Director

Acme Organization business continuity policy, Version 1                    Sept 2007

**Figure C.2 – Sample business continuity policy: Page 3**

# Appendix D.
# BCM competencies

The BCM team should demonstrate the ability to apply knowledge and skills in the areas listed below. The following competencies are based on those contained in *10 Standards Of Professional Competence* (The Business Continuity Institute, 2003).

## Initiation and management

- Establish and communicate the need for the business continuity management process.
- Establish stakeholders' interests.
- Establish a planning/steering committee, taking into account: roles and responsibilities, structure, control and development as well as membership.
- Develop budget and resource requirements.
- Identify business continuity team(s) and associated roles and responsibilities.
- Develop and co-ordinate action plans to develop and implement the BCM system.
- Develop the on going management and documentation requirements for the BCM system.
- Report to senior management and obtain senior management approval/commitment.
- Establish records management and control.

## Business impact analysis

- Understand BIA  (business impact analysis) methodologies.
- Understand assessment techniques: quantitative and qualitative methods.
- Establish the BIA process.
- Identify and implement information gathering activities.
- Assess effects of disruptions, loss exposure and business impact.
- Define criticality of business functions and processes, and prioritize recovery.
- Determine recovery time frames and minimum resource requirements.

## Risk assessment and control

- Understand loss potentials.
- Determine the organization's exposure to loss potentials.
- Evaluate, select and use appropriate risk analysis methodologies and tools.
- Identify controls and safeguards to prevent and/or mitigate the effects of loss potentials.
- Evaluate the effectiveness of controls and safeguards.

## Developing business continuity management strategies

- Identify enterprise-wide and business unit continuity strategic requirements.
- Assess suitability of alternative strategies against the results of a business impact analysis, risk assessment and recovery time objectives.
- Select appropriate continuity solutions.
- Prepare a cost/benefit analysis of continuity strategies and present findings to senior management.
- Understand contractual agreements for business continuity services.

## Co-ordination with external agencies

- Identify applicable laws and regulations governing emergency management.
- Identify and co-ordinate with agencies supporting business continuity needs and aims.
- Develop and facilitate appropriate exercises with external agencies.

## Incident response and operations

- Identify components of incident response.
- Develop detailed incident response procedures.
- Identify command and control requirements and procedures.
- Identify emergency response and triage requirements and procedures.
- Identify salvage and restoration requirements.

## Developing and implementing incident plans and business continuity management plans

- Determine plan development requirements.
- Define incident management and business continuity management control requirements.
- Identify and define the format and structure of major plan components.
- Draft plans.
- Define damage assessment/restoration strategy.
- Develop BCM team documentation.
- Develop business unit documentation.
- Develop information technology recovery team documentation.
- Develop communication systems.
- Implement plans.
- Establish plan distribution and control procedures.

## Incident communication

- Identify and develop a proactive incident communication programme.
- Establish essential incident communication plans with external agencies as appropriate.
- Establish essential communication plans with internal and external stakeholders to ensure they are kept informed in an appropriate manner.
- Establish essential incident communication plans with media outlets.
- Develop and facilitate exercises for incident communication plans.

## Maintaining and exercising plans

- Establish an exercise programme.
- Determine exercise requirements.
- Develop realistic scenarios.
- Establish exercise evaluation criteria and document findings.
- Create an exercise schedule.
- Prepare exercise control plan and reports.
- Facilitate exercises.
- Manage post-exercise reporting.
- Monitor actions resulting from exercise and feed back to appropriate people.
- Define plan maintenance scheme and schedule.
- Formulate change control procedures.
- Establish status reporting procedures.
- Audit objectives.

## Awareness and training programmes

- Define awareness and training objectives.
- Develop and deliver various types of training programmes as appropriate.
- Develop and deliver awareness programmes.
- Identify other opportunities for education.

# Appendix E.
# Establishing a training programme

People need training to equip them with the relevant knowledge and skills and to build relationships with other team players. Key questions to be asked in developing a training programme are listed below.

## Who needs to be trained?

- The BCM team.
- People named specifically in business continuity plans.
- Senior management.
- 'Non-essential' staff who may be needed at the time of plan invocation.
- Contractors and suppliers.

## How are training needs identified?

For every individual/group involved in delivering the BCMS (including those involved in plan invocation) the following should be listed.

## What do they need to know?

- Specific knowledge about role.
- General understanding of what others do.
- Processes used.

## What additional skills do they need?

- Specialist equipment skills.
- Interpersonal skills.

When answers have been obtained to the above questions, a training programme should be developed.

## Satisfying training needs

For every individual/group involved in delivering the BCMS (including those involved in plan invocation) it is important to identify any deficiencies in skills and knowledge in relation to those required to deliver the BCMS or invoke plans. This is sometimes called a gap analysis.

---

When deficiencies have been identified an appropriate training programme needs to be developed to bridge the gap.

## Training delivery

The training may use external or internal resources and should:

- develop skills through tutored practice as well as a self-development programme; possibly e-based;
- increase knowledge through discussion seminars and walk-through activities;
- build relationships by training with the team and through exercises.

Figure E.1 sets out a possible model for developing a training programme.

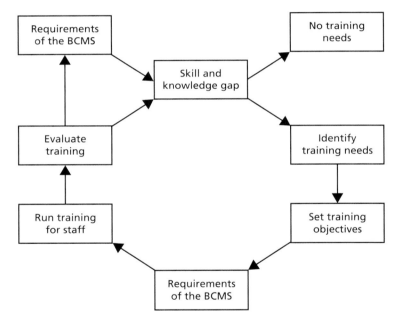

**Figure E.1 – Model for developing a training programme**

Effective training and validation requires a policy, commitment from the organization as well as the necessary resources. The training should be should be based on standards and targets and should also be subject to an assessment process.

It is essential to maintain a log of training for every identified individual or group involved in the BCM system.

# Appendix F.
# Stakeholder analysis template

| Stakeholder | Stakeholder's expectations | | Ranking |
| --- | --- | --- | --- |
| | Under normal circumstances | During a disruption | (high/med/low) |
| | | | |
| | | | |
| | | | |
| | | | |
| | | | |
| | | | |
| | | | |

Date of assessment ........................   Signed off by ...........................

Date to be reviewed ........................

Figure F.1 – Stakeholder analysis template for Acme Organization Ltd

# Appendix G.
# Business impact analysis template

Business impact analysis record for Acme Organization Ltd

| | Key services/products | Areas of impact (see below) | Impact (H/M/L) | Max tolerable period of disruption | Recovery time objective | Minimum service level |
|---|---|---|---|---|---|---|
| 1 | | | | | | |
| 2 | | | | | | |
| 3 | | | | | | |
| 4 | | | | | | |
| 5 | | | | | | |
| 6 | | | | | | |

**Business impact analysis template**

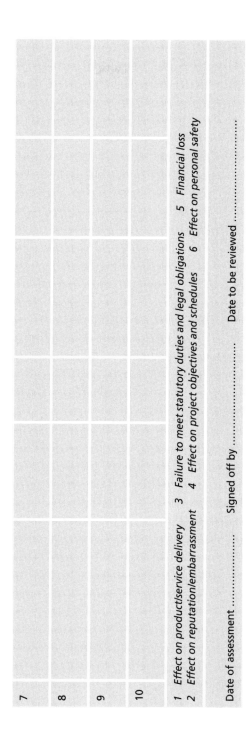

1 Effect on product/service delivery    3 Failure to meet statutory duties and legal obligations    5 Financial loss
2 Effect on reputation/embarrassment    4 Effect on project objectives and schedules    6 Effect on personal safety

Date of assessment ...............    Signed off by ...............    Date to be reviewed ...............

**Figure G.1 – Business impact analysis record for Acme Organization Ltd**

# Appendix H.
# Resource record

## Resource record for Acme Organization Ltd

| Service/activity | People | Skills | Computing equipment | Software applications | Telecommunications | Information/data | Non-ICT equipment | Accommodation | Furniture | Internal dependencies | Suppliers/partners |
|---|---|---|---|---|---|---|---|---|---|---|---|
| | | | | | | | | | | | |
| | | | | | | | | | | | |
| | | | | | | | | | | | |

**Resource record**

Date of assessment ...............       Signed off by ................       Date to be reviewed ................

**Figure H.1 – Resource record for Acme Organization Ltd**

# Appendix I.
# Risk mitigation record

## Risk mitigation measures for Acme Organization Ltd

Division/dept. .............................................  Key product/service ...........................................................

| Critical activity/resource/dependency | Risk | Ranking (H/M/L) | Risk mitigation measures |
|---|---|---|---|
|  |  |  |  |
|  |  |  |  |
|  |  |  |  |
|  |  |  |  |
|  |  |  |  |
|  |  |  |  |

The Route Map to Business Continuity Management

**Risk mitigation record**

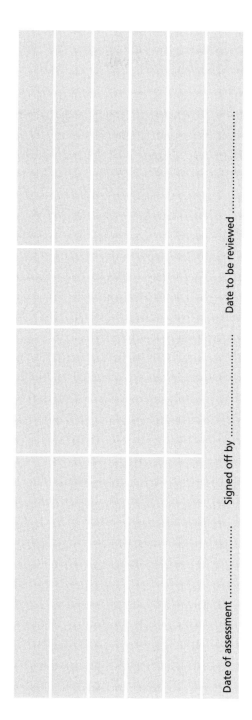

Date of assessment .............    Signed off by .............    Date to be reviewed .............

**Figure I.1 – Risk mitigation record for Acme Organization Ltd**

# Appendix J.
# Resource requirements template

| Division/dept. ................................ Key service/product ............................... | | | |
|---|---|---|---|
| | **Resource required** | | |
| | **0–24 hours*** | **Within 3 days*** | **Within 14 days*** |
| Activities that support key service/ product | | | |
| People and skills required | | | |
| Computing and telecoms required | | | |
| Software applications required | | | |
| Information required | | | |
| Non-ICT equipment required | | | |

| Accommodation required | | | |
|---|---|---|---|
| Furniture required | | | |
| Key suppliers/ partners | | | |
| Other dependencies | | | |
| Other comments | | | |

Date of assessment .............. Signed off by .............. Date to be reviewed ..............

* Timing set to suit organization's requirements

**Figure J.1 – Resource requirements for Acme Organization Ltd**

# Appendix K.
# Key resource strategies

The key resource strategies below are taken from BS 25999-1: 2006.

## People

'The organization should identify appropriate strategies for maintaining core skills and knowledge. This analysis should extend beyond employees to contractors and other stakeholders who possess extensive specialist skills and knowledge. Strategies to protect or provide those skills might include:

a) documentation of the way in which critical activities are performed;
b) multi-skill training of staff and contractors;
c) separation of core skills to reduce the concentration of risk (this might entail physical separation of staff with core skills or ensuring that more than one person has the requisite core skills);
d) use of third parties;
e) succession planning; and
f) knowledge retention and management.'

In setting the strategies in this area it is important to remember people will react differently during an emergency/major incident compared with how they operate normally.

## Premises

Worksite strategies can vary significantly and a range of options might be available. Different types of incident or threat might require the implementation of different or multiple worksite options. The correct strategies will in part be determined by the organization's size, sector and spread of activities, by stakeholders and by geographical base. For example, public authorities will need to maintain a frontline service delivery in their communities.

'The organization should devise a strategy for reducing the impact of the unavailability of its normal worksite(s). This may include one or more of the following:

a) alternative premises (locations) within the organization, including displacement of other activities;
b) alternative premises provided by other organizations (whether or not these are reciprocal arrangements);
c) alternative premises provided by third-party specialists [sometimes called work area recovery];

d) working from home or at remote sites;

e) other agreed suitable premises; and

f) use of an alternative workforce in an established site.

NOTE 1  If staff are to be moved to alternative premises, these premises ought to be close enough that staff are willing and able to travel there, taking into account any possible difficulties caused by the incident. However, the alternative premises ought not to be so close that they are likely to be affected by the same incident.

NOTE 2  The use of alternative premises for continuity purposes ought to be supported by a clear statement as to whether the alternative premises are for the sole use of the organization. If the alternative premises are shared with other organizations, a plan to mitigate the non-availability of these premises ought to be developed and documented.'

Another solution to relocating people to alternative premises is to provide them with remote access to IT via dial-up, or through the internet using Virtual Private Network (VPN) or similar technology.

'NOTE 3  It may be appropriate to move the workload rather than the staff, e.g. a manufacturing line or a call centre's workload.'

## Technology

Technology strategies will vary significantly between organizations according to the size, nature and complexity of business. Specific strategies ought to be developed to safeguard, replace or restore specialized or custom-built technologies with long lead times. The organization may need to make provision for manual operations before full technology services are recovered.

'Technology strategies will depend on the nature of the technology employed and its relationship to critical activities, but will typically be one or a combination of the following:

- provision made within the organization;
- services delivered to the organization; and
- services provided externally by a third party.

Technology strategies may include:

- geographical spread of technology, i.e. maintaining the same technology at different locations that will not be impacted by the same business disruption;
- holding older equipment as emergency replacement or spares; and
- additional risk mitigation for unique or long lead time equipment.

Information technology (IT) services frequently need complex continuity strategies. Where such strategies are required, consideration should be given to:

- recovery time objectives (RTOs) for systems and applications that support the key activities identified in the BIA;
- location and distance between technology sites;
- number of technology sites;
- remote access;
- the use of un-staffed (dark) sites as opposed to staffed sites;
- telecoms connectivity and redundant routing;
- the nature of 'failover' (whether manual intervention is required to activate alternative IT provision or whether this needs to occur automatically); and
- third-party connectivity and external links.'

## Information

'Information strategies should be such as to ensure that information vital to the organization's operation is protected and recoverable according to the timeframes described within the BIA.

Any information required for enabling the delivery of the organization's critical activities should have appropriate:

- confidentiality;
- integrity;
- availability; and
- currency.

Information strategies should be documented for the recovery of information that has not yet been copied or backed-up to a safe location.

Information strategies should extend to include:

- physical (hardcopy) formats; and
- virtual (electronic) formats, etc.

In all cases, information needs to be recovered to a point in time that is known and agreed by top management. Various methods of copying may be used, such as electronic or tape backups, microfiche, photocopies, creating dual copies at the time of production. This known recovery point is often referred to as the "recovery point objective".'

## Supplies

In office-based environments, supplies might constitute cheques, etc. Other industries might identify retail stock or just-in-time supplies, or vehicle fuels.

'The organization should identify and maintain an inventory of the core supplies that support its critical activities. Strategies to provide these may include:

- storage of additional supplies at another location;
- arrangements with third parties for delivery of stock at short notice;
- diversion of just-in-time deliveries to other locations;
- holding of materials at warehouses or shipping sites;
- transfer of sub-assembly operations to an alternative location that has supplies;
- identification of alternative/substitute supplies.

Where critical activities are dependent upon specialist suppliers or partners, the organization should identify the key suppliers and single sources of supply. Strategies to manage continuity of supply may include:

- increasing the number of suppliers;
- encouraging or requiring suppliers to have a validated business continuity capability;
- contractual and/or service level agreements with key suppliers;
- the identification of alternative, capable suppliers.'

# Appendix L.
## Sample incident log

| ACME ORGANIZATION LTD – INCIDENT LOG | | | | |
|---|---|---|---|---|
| INCIDENT .......... | LOCATION .......... | | LEAD MANAGER .......... | |
| IMPACTED SERVICES/PRODUCTS .......... | | | | |
| Date and time | Information/request | From | Action taken | By whom |
| | | | | |
| | | | | |
| | | | | |

**Sample incident log**

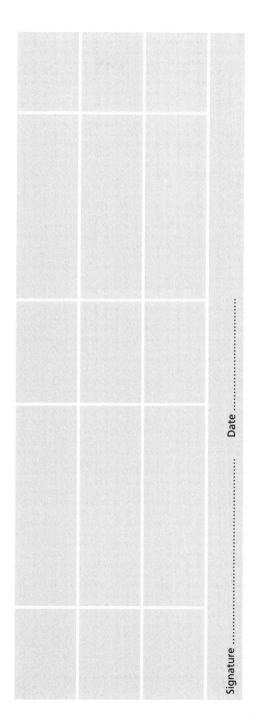

Signature ............................          Date ............................

**Figure L.1 – Incident log for Acme Organization Ltd**

# Appendix M.
# Sample business continuity plan

---

**ACME ORGANIZATION LTD –
HOME SERVICE MIDLAND DEPARTMENT**

**BUSINESS CONTINUITY PLAN – EMERGENCY CALL-OUT SERVICE**

Version 1:0 22/9/07

## Plan overview including ownership

### Business continuity plan – emergency call-out service

The aim of the plan is to enable the emergency call-out service of the Midland Home Service Department of the Home Services Division to be resumed following an event that disrupts the service. The emergency call-out service is a key service for the company as it is contracted to local housing associations.

Within two hours of a disruption the company must be able to receive and respond to emergency call-out requests from housing association tenants.

This plan assumes that the public telephone service has not been affected by the disruption.

This plan is owned by the Head of the Maintenance Department of the Home Service Division.

### Roles and responsibilities

The Business Unit Manager, or their deputy, is responsible for assessing the effects of a disruption and the impact on the capability of the unit to deliver the key service. If appropriate, the Business Unit Manager or their deputy will invoke this plan in order to restore the service to the agreed service level within the agreed timescale. The Business Unit Manager or their deputy will assemble their BCM team to implement the plan.

---

BCM Team members Position Contact Deputy Contact

Department BCM Co-ordinator
Deputy Dept. BCM Co-ordinator

Acme Organization BCM Manager
Deputy BCM Manager

## Notification, invocation and escalation rules

| | | |
|---|---|---|
| Major disruption that affects the whole of Acme Organization Ltd, e.g. denial of access to Acme head office complex. | Finance Director or nominated deputy to invoke corporate plan and assemble corporate BCM Team. | |
| Disruption that affects one division of Acme Organization Ltd, e.g. loss of key staff across division. | Head of division or deputy to invoke plan, assemble department BCM Team and inform BCM Manager or deputy. | If disruption proves to be wider than department then head of division or deputy escalates to BCM Manager. |
| Disruption that affects one business unit, e.g. vehicles unavailable for service engineers. | Business Unit Manager or deputy to invoke plan, assemble BCM Team and inform Divisional BCM Co-ordinator. | If disruption proves to be wider than business unit then Business Unit Manager or deputy escalates to head of division. |

*Command centre details*

If required the BCM team will assemble in the second floor meeting room of the Midlands office. If this location is not available the alternative location for the command centre is the welfare room at the vehicle garage on Lichfield Street.

Contact details of command centres:

Insert map of command centre locations

Command centre location: Midlands office

Alternative:  Garage, Lichfield St.

Facilities at command centres include telephone, internet access, battle box.

Battle box contains:

*Contacts, internal and external*

- Internal
- External
- Subject experts

*Task checklists*

- Mandatory tasks ...................................................................................
  ...................................................................................................
- Discretionary tasks ..............................................................................
  ...................................................................................................
- Task completion tracking process – record all actions taken, together with times, on the action/task worksheet.

## Critical activities recovery plans

- Schedule of critical activities including recovery times and levels.
- Recovery plans for critical activities.
- Recovery site location(s).

*Example*

Minimum of two maintenance engineers to be available within two hours, operating from home if unable to operate out of normal office location or recovery location.

In the event of no staff being available then mutual aid arrangements are in place with Any Job Any Where Any Time Company. Contact details are listed above.

Mutual aid plan is as follows: ...............................................................

*Recovery resource requirements*

- People
- Information/data
- IT
- Telecommunications
- Vehicles

- Specialist equipment
- Accommodation
- Office equipment
- Furniture
- Stationery, etc.

*The following supporting information not included in the plan is located as shown*

- Personnel records                                      } – HR Department
- Handling injuries and fatalities                       }
- Staff welfare and counselling                          }
- Health and safety                                      }

- Communicating with staff                               } – Corporate Communications
- Handling the media and PR                              }

- Emergency services liaison                             } – Building Management

- Finance                                                }
- Insurance policies                                     } – Corporate Finance Department
- Legal advice                                           }

- Communicating with suppliers and intermediaries }
- Supplier agreements                                    } – Purchasing Department

*Form templates*

- Meetings agenda
- Decision and action log
- Task list status report
- Telephone log

Plan signed off by ..................................... Head of Home Service Division

Date to be reviewed .....................................

**Figure M.1 – Business continuity plan for Acme Organization Ltd**

# Appendix N.
# Self-assessment questionnaire

## Suggested BCMS self-assessment checklist

Rate achievement for each key issue (1 – not started, 2 – 25 per cent complete, 3 – 50 per cent complete, 4 – 75 per cent complete, 5 – completed)

Table N.1 – BCMS self-assessment checklist

| Stages | Key issues | Example evidence | Rating |
|---|---|---|---|
| **BCM programme** | Responsibility for business continuity management issues is clearly defined within the organization at the corporate management level. | Named executive director accountable for BCM policy and implementation. Reports to senior management groups. | 1-2-3-4-5 |
| | BCM Manager or Co-ordinator appointed. | Named individual in post responsible for implementing and maintaining the BCM programme. | 1-2-3-4-5 |
| | A BCMS is formalized through the organization's policy and procedures. | A BCM policy and scoping documents exist. The BCM policy is published internally and externally. | 1-2-3-4-5 |

**Self-assessment questionnaire**

| Stages | Key issues | Example evidence | Rating |
|---|---|---|---|
| | Responsibility for business continuity issues is well embedded within individual services or management units. | BCM is included in job descriptions and skill sets of service and support managers. BCM responsibilities enforced by inclusion in organization's appraisal, reward and recognition policies. | 1-2-3-4-5 |
| | Awareness of business continuity issues is well embedded throughout the organization. | There is a programme in place for raising awareness throughout the organization and among its key stakeholders. Feedback mechanisms exist through which functional managers and staff can flag up BCM issues as evidenced by minutes of meetings and reports. Induction programmes include awareness of BCM. | 1-2-3-4-5 |
| | Assurance of organization's BCM capability | KPIs set for BCM implementation and maintenance. BCM responsibilities reviewed through the organization's audit process. | 1-2-3-4-5 |
| Understanding the organization | Identification of the organization's objectives, stakeholder obligations, statutory and regulatory duties and the environment in which the organization operates. | Analysis carried out of stakeholder obligations and expectations. Statutory and regulatory duties listed. | 1-2-3-4-5 |
| | Key services and products delivered by and on behalf of the organization have been identified and have been agreed by the executive board. | Procedures for identifying and reviewing key services and products have been documented. Executive board minutes confirm key services and products. | 1-2-3-4-5 |

**Self-assessment questionnaire**

| Stages | Key issues | Example evidence | Rating |
|---|---|---|---|
| | Critical functions, processes and supporting resources required to deliver key services and products, within and without the organization, have been identified. | Documentation has been produced detailing critical functions, processes and supporting resources. Mapping undertaken of critical suppliers and partners. | 1-2-3-4-5 |
| | Identification of the impact over time on the organization and its stakeholders of the loss of any key service or product. | A structured business impact analysis (BIA) process exists for the organization that prioritizes key services and products. A documented BIA has been drawn up covering the key services and products of the organization. Executive board minutes confirm BIA. | 1-2-3-4-5 |
| | Risk assessment has been used on the critical activities and supporting resources to focus effort on the areas of greatest need. | Procedures have been documented to review and rank risk. 'Single points of failure' identified. | 1-2-3-4-5 |
| | Countermeasures exist to minimize risks that have been identified, including measures to combat potential loss of information. | Evidence of risk mitigation covering people, systems, information, premises, equipment and suppliers has been documented. | 1-2-3-4-5 |
| **Determining business continuity strategies** | Development of appropriate strategies to limit, over time, the impact of the loss of key services and products on the organization and its stakeholders. | Strategies documented to support each key service and product. Strategies cover people, premises, technology, information, suppliers and stakeholders. Strategies take account of actions taken by public services in an emergency situation. Executive board minutes confirm strategy selection and their required resource allocations. | 1-2-3-4-5 |

The Route Map to Business Continuity Management

**Self-assessment questionnaire**

| Stages | Key issues | Example evidence | Rating |
|---|---|---|---|
| | Development of strategies to minimize supplier disruption. | Procurement policies created for key suppliers that require BCM to be incorporated into supply contracts. Evidence of BCM included in supply contracts. Alternative suppliers identified. | 1-2-3-4-5 |
| **Developing and implementing a BCM response** | Incident management plans are developed. Generic business continuity plans are developed that are flexible enough to maintain continuity of key services and products through a range of disruptive events. | Structure and procedures for developing incident and business continuity plans produced. Reports written. Minutes of planning meetings kept. Plans are clear, unambiguous and easy to use. Evidence of consultation with relevant staff in functional units and incorporation of feedback during plan development has been documented. Plans identify objectives, personnel involved, and command and control arrangements. Plans contain references to other sources of relevant information, advice and other documentation. | 1-2-3-4-5 |
| | A clear procedure exists for invoking the plans and delivering the response. | Invocation and response procedures documented. Key staff are identified in plans. Call-out lists exist for incident and continuity team members. | 1-2-3-4-5 |
| | Plans have clear ownership and are signed off at the appropriate level. | It is clear who is responsible for ensuring that each section/department or site has plans. All plans are signed. | 1-2-3-4-5 |

**Self-assessment questionnaire**

| Stages | Key issues | Example evidence | Rating |
|--------|-----------|------------------|--------|
| | Appointment of teams that are trained to deliver the plans. | Details recorded of incident and continuity team members. Training programme created for team members. Training record kept for team members. | 1-2-3-4-5 |
| | A clear procedure exists that ensures internal and external stakeholders are aware of what actions the organization will take if plans are activated. | A communications policy document exists. Letters, emails, circulars, meeting minutes, internet and intranet pages raise awareness of the plans. | 1-2-3-4-5 |
| | Communication with stakeholders at the time of disruption to key services and products ensured. | Plans contain arrangements for communicating with clients, customers, staff, stakeholders, partners and the media. Plans are linked to communication plans. | 1-2-3-4-5 |
| | Ensure latest plans and supporting materials are always available. | Copies of plans and essential equipment/ documents (in electronic or hard copy) are easily available on and off-site. All plans are subject to document and version control processes. | 1-2-3-4-5 |
| | Plans linked to other event plans within and without the organization. | Links to emergency plans, recovery plans, major incident plans, communication plans, etc. are documented. | 1-2-3-4-5 |
| Exercising | Ensure there is a balanced programme of exercise types that validates the full range of BCM capabilities. | Records exist of regularly tested contact arrangements and exercises. Exercise programmes/ test schedules exist. | 1-2-3-4-5 |
| | Exercise programmes have clear objectives. | Exercise scenarios and plans have been developed. | 1-2-3-4-5 |

The Route Map to Business Continuity Management

**Self-assessment questionnaire**

| Stages | Key issues | Example evidence | Rating |
|---|---|---|---|
| | Risk and impact assessments have been applied to the exercise. | Assessments are documented. | 1-2-3-4-5 |
| | Ensure there is a documented process for capturing and taking forward the lessons identified. | Notes of exercise debriefs kept, 'lessons learned' reports produced. Exercise review report sent to relevant management team. Action plans created. Actions reviewed at plan preparation and plan review meetings. Evidence that lessons learned from exercises have been incorporated into plans has been documented. | 1-2-3-4-5 |
| Maintaining | Ensure that the plans are kept up to date | There is an established and documented plan review process. Plan review is built into the business planning cycle. Notes from review meetings kept. Version controlled updates and acknowledgment systems for recipients issued. | 1-2-3-4-5 |
| | Ensure that when major changes occur within the organization or to the environment in which it operates, or threat levels change, the organization's BCM programme is reviewed and modified as appropriate. | There is a mechanism to identify and trigger BCM review points. Notes from review meetings kept. Action plans made. Review of actions has taken place at plan preparation/review meetings. | 1-2-3-4-5 |

Self-assessment questionnaire

| Stages | Key issues | Example evidence | Rating |
|--------|-----------|------------------|--------|
| **Reviewing** | A clear mechanism is in place for measuring the effectiveness of the business continuity management system. | BCMS review programme created. Self-assessment reports produced. Internal audit reports exist. Benchmarking carried out against standards (e.g. BS 25999) and guidelines. External reviews undertaken by peers from other organizations. | 1-2-3-4-5 |
| | Ensure that the review process drives improvement by identifying lessons and taking appropriate action. | Review process reports to relevant management team. Action plans produced. Review of actions takes place at BCMS review meetings. Evidence exists showing that the lessons learned from reviews have been incorporated into the organization's BCMS. | 1-2-3-4-5 |

# References

BS 25999-1:2006, *Business continuity management – Part 1: Code of practice*, London: British Standards Institution

BS 25999-2:2007, *Business continuity management – Part 2: Specification*, London: British Standards Institution

BS EN ISO 9001:2000, *Quality management systems – Requirements*, London: British Standards Institution

BS EN ISO 14001:2004, *Environmental management systems – Requirements with guidance for use*, London: British Standards Institution

Chartered Management Institute (2005) *Business Continuity Management 2005*, London: Chartered Management Institute

Chartered Management Institute (2006) *Business Continuity Management 2006*, London: Chartered Management Institute

Chartered Management Institute (2007) *Business Continuity Management 2007*, London: Chartered Management Institute

Great Britain (2004) *Civil Contingencies Act 2004*, London: The Stationery Office

HM Government (2005) *Emergency Preparedness, Guidance on Part 1 of the Civil Contingencies Act 2004*, London: UK Cabinet Office

Knight, R F and Pretty, D J (2000) *The Impact of Catastrophes on Shareholder Value*, Oxford: Templeton College, University of Oxford

PAS 56:2003, *Guide to business continuity management*, London: British Standards Institution (PAS 56:2003 is now withdrawn. Please see BS 25999-1:2006)

Porter, E M (1998) *Competitive Advantage*. New York: Simon & Schuster

Sharp, J (1999) *The Unifying Process*, Caversham: The Business Continuity Institute

The Business Continuity Institute (2003) *10 Standards of Professional Competence*, Caversham: The Business Continuity Institute

Turnbull, N et al. (1999) *Internal Control – Guidance for Directors on the Combined Code*, London: Institute of Chartered Accountants in England and Wales. Available at: http://www.icaew.co.uk/internalcontrol